Abstracting
and indexing
2nd edition

By the same author

Computers for libraries 2nd edition
1985. ISBN 0-85157-388-6

The basics of information technology
1988. ISBN 0-85157-396-7

Abstracting
and indexing

2nd edition

JENNIFER E. ROWLEY

CLIVE BINGLEY  LONDON

Published by
Clive Bingley Limited
7 Ridgmount Street
London WC1E 7AE

First published 1982
Second edition 1988
Reprinted 1990

British Library Cataloguing in Publication Data

Rowley, J. E.
   Abstracting and indexing.
   1. Documents. Abstracting. 2. Documents. Subject indexing
   I. Title
   025.4'8

   ISBN 0-85157-411-4

Typeset in 10/12pt Times by Library Association Publishing Ltd.
Printed and made in Great Britain by Billing and Sons Ltd, Worcester

CONTENTS

INTRODUCTION

Document analysis makes a significant contribution to communication and information flow. There are two major document analysis tools: abstracts and indexes. Students need to understand both how to produce these, and why and where they are appropriate. Some students of librarianship and information science will find themselves employed as abstractors and indexers. Many others will be engaged in the evaluation, acquisition and exploitation of information tools that rely upon abstracts and indexes, such as printed abstracting and indexing publications and computerized databases. An appreciation of the decisions necessary in the compilation of abstracts and indexes is essential not only to the intending indexer but also to the information staff devoted to information work.

Abstracting and indexing data are a vital component in the communication link between the originator of information and its ultimate consumer. Abstracts and indexes organize the literature so that a specialist can identify documents of interest more easily. This has long been recognized as important in science and technology. More recently, organization of the literature has been recognized as important in business and management, the social sciences, economics, and various other areas within the arts and humanities. Document analysis is, then, a universal tool.

This work is not a comprehensive account of all abstracting and indexing practice; space dictates that it be selective. Instead, the author has attempted to present a readable account of some of the key practices in the twin fields of abstracting and indexing. Central practices are highlighted and should lay a firm foundation for more advanced studies. This book also attempts to lay the groundwork for abstracting and indexing practice. A trainee indexer or abstractor must practise and refine these techniques, but this book should prepare the student for such practice. Practice is paramount. Only such theory as is necessary to an intelligent application of techniques is covered, and other texts should be consulted for further theoretical treatment. Thus, many of the more sophisticated techniques with limited potential for application are omitted. Space has rather been devoted to a more thorough treatment of a relatively limited number of techniques.

The approach taken in the book should appeal to students of library and information science. Others engaged in organizing and exploiting information, such as managers, computer scientists and administrators, should also find something of interest.

The work assumes a knowledge of basic cataloguing and classification practices in its readers. Although this background is not essential, a more integrated understanding of the organization of knowledge and information retrieval will be achieved in the presence of this knowledge. Familiarity with the description of documents, the formulation of author headings, simple alphabetical subject headings and the major classification schemes are useful prerequisites.

An attempt has been made to achieve an integrated view of manual and computerized information-retrieval systems and abstracting products. Both computerized and manual information-retrieval systems have a contribution to make to the organization of knowledge although, since the first edition of this book, the number and type of environments where manual systems persist have become much more limited. Nevertheless, printed abstracting and indexing journals are still sold in significant numbers, and are used by those who either do not have ready access to computer databases, or prefer to use the printed product. Furthermore, as far as the techniques of automatic indexing and automatic abstracting are concerned, there is still progress to be made before these can replace manual indexing and abstracting. Automatic indexing is better established in real applications than automatic abstracting, but even in environments where computer indexing is available, human indexers often intervene to improve upon the pure computer indexing. These topics are explored more fully at the appropriate places later in the book.

Necessarily, many ideas are omitted from this work, but then this is perhaps its strength. Scant attention is paid to evaluation and the needs of users. Little in general is said about the retrieval side of the systems; document analysis has stolen the limelight. Omission does not imply that those areas are not important. It was deemed appropriate to focus on specific topics and leave other topics to other authors. This selective approach proved popular in the first edition of this work, and it has been retained in this second edition. The second edition, then, adheres to the same basic structure as the first edition, although significant changes of emphasis in some areas of abstracting and indexing practice have necessitated substantial revision of some parts of this text.

Acknowledgements

The author wishes to acknowledge her debt to the authors of the literature that has gone before, and also to the various persons and organizations that have kindly permitted the reproduction of their work. The author is also grateful to Mrs D. Martin for her work in typing parts of the manuscript of this text.

Chapter 1

COMPUTERS AND ABSTRACTING AND INDEXING

The twin processes of abstracting and indexing, as covered in this book, are practices and procedures that people enact. They can be described without reference to computers. However, the reality is that these processes are often associated with the creation of input to a computer system, and it is not sufficient merely to describe the processes that govern the creation and generation of indexing and abstracting data. Indexing and abstracting are performed for a purpose. The products that are produced from indexing and abstracting data are discussed in greater detail in Chapter 10. In order to select and apply the most appropriate abstracting and indexing techniques, it is necessary to examine the way in which the indexing and abstracting data are used. In other words, although our focus in this text is on the first stage in the following diagram, we must pay some attention to the later stages, in order to understand and evaluate aspects of the first stage:

Creation of indexing ⟶ Store ⟶ Products
and abstracting data

This book attempts to treat computerized and non-computerized information-retrieval systems in an integrated manner. Nevertheless, in most cases the 'store' for the abstracting and indexing data is a computer. In order to appreciate fully some of the aspects of abstracting and, more specifically, indexing practice, that are introduced in later chapters, it is necessary to have some grasp of some fundamental aspects of computerized information-retrieval systems.

This chapter introduces those features of computerized information-retrieval systems that are essential to an understanding of the chapters that follow. For a full introduction to computer systems, the reader should peruse one of the many interesting introductory texts on this subject.

Indexing and abstracting data will usually be input into a database held in a computer system. The database may be bibliographic (storing references to documents available elsewhere) or non-bibliographic (storing facts, figures, text or graphics). This chapter introduces the concepts of records, files and databases. Information is held in *files* or *databases*, which are comprised of *records*, which in turn are comprised of *fields*

1

or *data items*, which again may be comprised of *subfields* or *data elements*.

1.1 Records

A record is a complete unit of information about a person, item, product, book, patient, chemical, etc. Our focus in this book is on bibliographic records which contain information about documents such as books, periodical articles, conference proceedings, theses, reports, standards and patents. A file will comprise a number of records about, say, different documents, but each record will contain similar information about its document. Records are normally divided into fields. Each record in a file will have the same fields in it, although data may not necessarily always be entered in each field. Figure 1.1 shows the fields in some typical bibliographic records, whilst Figure 1.2 shows the fields in some non-bibliographic records.

Fig. 1.1   Some sample bibliographic records

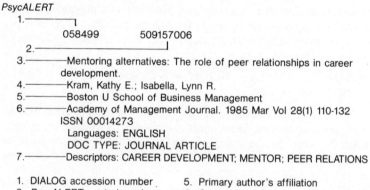

PsycALERT

1. ─────┐
   058499   509157006
2. ───────────────────┘
3. ──────Mentoring alternatives: The role of peer relationships in career development.
4. ──────Kram, Kathy E.; Isabella, Lynn R.
5. ──────Boston U School of Business Management
6. ──────Academy of Management Journal. 1985 Mar Vol 28(1) 110-132
   ISSN 00014273
   Languages: ENGLISH
   DOC TYPE: JOURNAL ARTICLE
7. ──────Descriptors: CAREER DEVELOPMENT; MENTOR; PEER RELATIONS

1. DIALOG accession number
2. PsycALERT control number
3. Article title
4. Author(s)

5. Primary author's affiliation
6. Source journal
7. Indexing terms and keyword descriptors

BIS Informat

AN: 1000500   PIN:1000500   JA:850103   UP:8501
TI: BRITISH AEROSPACE – SALES OPPORTUNITIES IN INDONESIA
JN: Financial Times   PD:850103 PG:4
GC: UK,INDO GL:United Kingdom, Indonesia AR:United Kingdom and Ireland, South East Asia AC:UK,SEA

TY: TRA CL:ELMIL
TD: Trade MH:Military Communications

Fig. 1.1 continued

AB: BA, which signed a $120 deal to supply a Rapier missile system to the Indonesian Army in Dec 1984, is now looking at other sales opportunities in the country, especially selling aircraft to the Indonesian Air Force. At present, Indonesia depends for most of its air defence on three squadrons of Skyhawks. These will need replacing before the end of the decade. There is, however, a strong pressure group within the military that is pressing for the more sophisticated supersonic American F-16 fighter. Another possible sales area for British companies is the Indonesian Navy. There are thought to be opportunities for the sale of British minesweepers and a variety of radar and electronic equipment – earlier this year Britain sold three re-fitted frigates to the Indonesian Navy for $40m (£26.6m).

AN	Accession Number	TY	Type Heading
TI	Title	TD	Company
JN	Journal Name	AB	Abstract
GC	Geographical Code		

INSPEC

Accession Nos	B86052872, C86043681
Title	Microcomputer for the dynamics laboratory
Author	Martin, J.; Kim, J.
Affiliation	Mech.Eng., New Jersey Inst.of Technol., Newark, NJ, USA
Journal	Microprocess.& Microsyst. (GB) vol. 10, no.4 216-21
Publication Date	May 1986
Coden	MIMID5
ISSN	0141-9331
Document Type	Journal Paper
Language	English
Treatment Code	Practical
Abstract	A microcomputer developed for use in a dynamics laboratory of a mechanical engineering department is discussed. The microcomputer is based on the Motorola 6802 micro-processor and includes an EPROM burning circuit for flexibility. Special mathematical routines have been developed for the computer. These routines are designed for use with 4-digit floating-point numbers to gain speed with minimal sacrifice of accuracy. The special routines include a data approximation and smoothing routine for signal processing, and routines to compute frequency used mathematical function. The routines are written in 6802 assembly language and are stored in 2 kbyte of external EPROM. An application of the microcomputer used as a component in a speed controller is also discussed.

Fig. 1.1 continued

Controlled Terms	computerised control; mechanical engineering computing; microcomputer applications; microcomputers; velocity control
Uncontrolled Terms	microcomputer; dynamics laboratory; mechanical engineering department; Motorola 6802 microprocessor; EPROM burning circuit; flexibility; mathematical routines; 4-digit floating-point numbers; data approximation; smoothing routine; signal processing; 6802 assembly language; speed controller
Classification	B1265F; C5430; C7420; C7440

Further examination of Figure 1.1 will show that a bibliographic record can usually accommodate an abstract, a bibliographic citation (giving data to assist in the location of the original document to which the record pertains) and indexing terms. There may be only one type of indexing term used, but some files have records with several distinct fields for different kinds of indexing terms, such as classification codes, alphabetical indexing terms and subject headings. In addition to these fields, which clearly incorporate indexing data, a number of other fields in the record may be exploited in retrieval. These may include author's name, source reference, title, abstract, to give just a few examples. Retrieval is explored further in later chapters. It is sufficient to observe at this point that:

- the data in some fields act primarily as a retrieval device
- the data in some fields are recorded for eventual display when the record is shown on the screen
- the data in some fields serve both of the above functions.

1.2 Fields

One of the most important characteristics of fields is whether they are fixed- or variable-length fields.

Fixed-length fields have a specified allocation of characters. The data entered into a fixed-length field may be of variable length, but cannot exceed the pre-defined length of the field. Fixed-length fields are useful for fixed-length data such as codes and numbers, but do not acommodate variable-length data satisfactorily. If variable-length data (e.g. a title) are to be entered into a fixed-length field, there will be occasions when there is spare capacity in the field, and others when the length of data will exceed that of the field. Fixed-length fields have attractions for ease of retrieval. Since the length of a field and its position in a record is constant for all records, the computer need be instructed only once concerning the location of the field. Software to cater for variable-length fields needs to be more complex.

Fig. 1.2   Some sample non-bibliographic records

Harvard Business Review database

HBRO 1971-OCT 1985
  The Heart of Entrepreneurship
  Stevenson. Howard H.. Gumpert. David E.
  HARVARD BUSINESS REVIEW. Mar-Apr 1985.
  p.85.

Abstract:
Organizations that encourage executives to strike
out and create new products will best adapt
and prosper in a rapidly changing world. But
matching an individual's interest in entrepreneurship with company needs and goals is
no easy task. Entrepreneurship can be viewed
in the context of a range of behavior. At one
extreme is the promoter type of manager. who
feels confident of his or her ability to seize
opportunity. This manager expects . . .

Bibliographic citation and abstract

HBRO 1971-OCT 1985
  The Heart of Entrepreneurship
  Stevenson. Howard H.. Gumpert. David E.
  HARVARD BUSINESS REVIEW. Mar-Apr 1985.
  p.85.

Text:
Single-minded capital allocation systems.
They assume that the consequences of future
uncertainty can be measured now. or at least
that uncertainty a year from now will be no less
than that at present. Thus a single decision
point seems appropriate. Many capital budget
systems make it difficult to get two bites of
an apple.

Full text of the document

Kirk-Othmer Online

Kirk-Othmer Encyclopedia of Chemical Technology
Third Edition. Full Text
Copyright John Wiley & Sons. Inc

nicotine same *exposure*

Result 2 Documents
Colloids.
Kirk-Othmer 3rd ed.Vol 25.241-259.
Bleier-A.

Table 6. *Exposure* limits of Selected Colloidal
Materials
Column Headings (2):
(1) Substance
(2) Limit. mg/m**3

(1)	(2)
asbestos	70.6
boron oxide	15
cadmium dust	7
nicotine	0.5

temperatures with *fluorosilicone* adj *elastomers*

Result 2 Documents
Fluorine Compounds.Organic—Poly(fluoro-
  silicones).
Kirk-Othmer.3rd ed.Vol 11.74-82.
Kim-Y-K.
Dow Corning Corporation.

1
TX 7 OF 38.
  Heat Resistance. *Fluorosilicone elastomers*
  give long-lasting dependability in both
  static and dynamic applications over a wide
  temperature range. Most

ICC companies database—ICCF: First part of a full-text record

AN	00052457 8510 Full Record.	
CO	CADBURY SCHWEPPES PUBLIC LIMITED COMPANY	
	Public Limited Company	
RO	Registered Office: 1-4 CONNAUGHT PLACE	
	LONDON	
	W2 2EX	
HI	Accounts Reference Date: 12/31	

Fig. 1.2 continued

Date of latest Accounts: 841229
Date of last Annual Return: 850516
Date of Incorporation: 970506
Company Status: Live Company
Date Dissolved: 000000
History: 850513: change of directors: 850305: plc's share allotment returns
Quoted: Yes
Accounts lodge name: CADBURY SCHWEPPES PLC
Auditors: Arthur Andersen & Co/Arthur Young

IN   Trading Address: 1-4 Connaught Place
               London
               W2 2EX

MM Secretary: M H Hayman.
Director(s): N C Bain: H J M Blakeney: Sir Adrian Cadbury: N D Cadbury: H R Collum: B C Dice: H Lavery: T J Organ: P H Reay: and others.

PN The manufacture and sale of confectionery, soft drinks, beverages, foods and household products.

CC (4214) Cocoa, chocolate and sugar confectionery:(6170) Wholesale distribution of food, drink and tobacco: (4239) Miscellaneous foods: (4283) Soft drinks.

SC AAA:BRE:CCE:FPE:ZFP.

FF Consolidated Data (000's ukl)
Subsidiary Company: No

Date of Accounts	841231	831231	830101	820103
Number of Weeks	52	52	52	52
Balance Sheet:				
Fixed Assets	599,400	504,100	441,300	323,900
Intangible Assets				
Intermediate Assets	33,100	28,800	23,400	15,900
Stocks	316,600	266,900	265,700	187,500
Debtors	285,300	244,600	202,200	192,500
Other Current Assets	103,800	96,200	122,100	136,800
Total Current Assets	705,700	607,700	590,000	516,800
Creditors	218,300	154,000	105,700	213,800
Short Term Loans	55,500	96,900	89,000	53,200
Other Current Liab	257,400	217,700	222,700	49,500
Total Current Liab	531,200	468,600	417,400	316,500
Net Assets	807,000	672,000	637,300	540,100
Total Assets	1,338,200	1,140,600	1,054,700	856,600
Shareholders Funds	518,700	399,900	389,600	384,200
Long Term Loans	202,200	190,900	178,200	125,600
Other Long Term Liab	86,100	81,200	69,500	30,300
Capital Employed	807,000	672,000	637,300	540,100
Profit/Loss:				
Sales	2,016,200	1,702,800	1,494,200	1,271,000
U.K. Sales	NA	NA	NA	NA
Exports	NA	NA	NA	NA
Profits	124,000	106,900	89,700	80,600
Interest Paid	48,700	36,000	34,500	25,200
Directors Remuneration	1,508	1,349	1,171	863
Employees Remuneration	342,400	309,600	277,000	137,600
No. of Employees	35,455	37,140	38,148	23,384

Variable-length fields are fields where the length of any given field varies from one record to another. Normally, the length of the field will be the length of the data to be entered into the field. Variable-length fields, then, are good for variable-length data, such as names, titles, notes, abstracts and full text. Variable-length fields lead to compact storage, but the computer needs to be told where data can be found in each record. Fields may be labelled by:

(a) field delimiters and labels. Field labels are characters that identify specific fields. A field delimiter marks the end of a field.
(b) directory format. A computer-generated directory accompanies each record. The directory records the location of each field in any given record.

1.3 Record structures

A structured record, split into fields and, if necessary, subfields, facilitates the easy retrieval and rearrangement of the contents of the records for display and printing. A bibliographic citation, together with abstract, could be recorded in a computer system without being split into fields, but individual fields in records allow these to be identified and separately manipulated, so that it is possible, for example, to:

● search on specific record sets
● search on specific fields
● sort according to specific fields
● print/display specific fields.

There are a number of standard record formats that are encountered in library and information work. Probably the most important are the MARC record format and the UNIBID record format. The MARC record format is employed in national, international and local cataloguing databases. The UNIBID record format has been designed for application in databases associated with abstracting and indexing journals.

Many national, international and local databases do not adhere to any standard record format structure. A standard structure is useful in exchanging records between different agencies, but may not always be appropriate to local requirements. The design of a record format is part of the task of systems design, and the local needs must be analysed before designing a record format.

1.4 Files

A file or database is a collection of similar records. These records will be arranged in some order so that it is possible to access individual records or sets of records.

Before exploring file organization any further, it is important to distinguish between logical and physical records. Records relating to a specific entity, e.g. a specific indexing term, are logical records. The file media on which they are stored are the physical storage media, e.g. magnetic disc or tape, and the physical arrangement of records on the storage media is distinct from the user's logical perception of records. The logical data structure is the structure that is important to the computer-system user.

The following types of data structure are common:

(a) *hierarchical*, or tree, with a single root element at the top, plus node elements at the ends of the branches that spread out from the root. Searching through a hierarchical structure moves from top to bottom.
(b) *network*, which is similar to a hierarchy, but here each node can have more than one owner and movement between nodes can be in either direction.
(c) *relational*, where all information is held in a form that can be represented by two-dimensional tables. The relationship of a record in one table to a record in another is indicated by having similar fields in each table. The tables are called 'relations'.
(d) an *inverted file*, which is a way of having efficient searches of certain types of files when searching for a particular attribute. An inverted file is similar to an index, and is common in information-retrieval applications.

Figure 1.3 shows some of these file structures diagrammatically.

Fig. 1.3 Some examples of database file structures

A hierarchical file structure

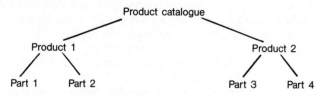

A network file structure

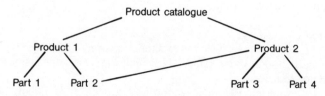

Fig. 1.3 continued

A relational file

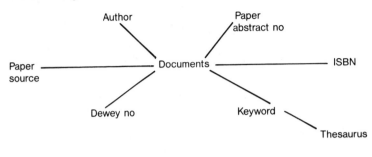

This brief chapter has introduced the way in which abstracting and indexing data are formatted for and stored in computer-based information-retrieval systems. These ideas are further amplified by subsequent chapters, especially chapters 7, 8, 9, and 10. These chapters go on to examine the ways in which the data, once structured and stored, can be retrieved and used to produce a range of information products.

Chapter 2

ABSTRACTS

Abstracts are an important component of many primary and secondary publications, current-awareness services and computerized databases. This chapter opens the topic of abstracts and abstracting by discussing the various kinds of abstracts and their functions.

2.1 What is an abstract?

A simple definition of an abstract is a useful starting point:

> An abstract is a concise and accurate representation of the contents of a document, in a style similar to that of the original document.

Although the term abstract is used with slightly differing meanings in different contexts and by different people, it is usually expected that an abstract will cover all the main points made in the original document, and follow the style and arrangement of the parent document. Abstracts, unless specified otherwise, are non-critical. Absence of criticism is a necessary prerequisite of a style which aims to report, but not comment upon, the content of the original. Abstracts are self-contained and complete. They assume only that the reader has some knowledge of the subject, but not that he will necessarily have the opportunity to peruse the original.

We will pause for a moment to distinguish between an abstract and various other document abridgements and surrogates. Although all surrogates facilitate communication, each type of surrogate is designed to serve a distinct purpose, and the boundary between the various types of document surrogates is not always clearly defined. Terms are not always used consistently or in accordance with the descriptions given below. However, the subsequent discussion should at least serve to illustrate the variety of approaches to the preparation of a document abridgement or surrogate.

Let us start with the *annotation*. An annotation is a note added to the title and/or other bibliographic information of a document by way of comment or explanation. In a cataloguing context the term is often used to refer to the notes which are appended to the standard bibliographic description of a document, as part of that document's entry in a catalogue.

Such an annotation may include comments on any element of the bibliographic description, including, for example, previous publication history, special features of physical format, subject content, earlier titles and related works. Annotations found in bibliographies may be less stylized and, although they also may cover any of the previously mentioned details, are more likely to dwell on the subject content. In this sense, an annotation in a bibliography is closer to an abstract. Indeed, much of Chapter 3 is equally applicable to the preparation of good annotations. Nevertheless, an annotation is basically an expansion of the information given in the bibliographic citation. Its objectives are more limited than those of an abstract, and consequently, in general, an annotation will be briefer than an abstract.

Another means of document representation is the *extract*. An extract is one or more portions of a document selected to represent the whole document. Plainly, in many documents sections that can be regarded as truly representative of the flavour of the original are absent or difficult to identify. The contents of an extract will often be culled from the results, conclusions or recommendations, i.e. the concluding segments, of the document. Due to the very nature of these portions they are unlikely to be a balanced representation of the whole document, but will tend to highlight certain significant points made in the document.

A third type of document abridgement is the *summary*. The distinction between a summary and an abstract is often not clearly indicated. Strictly, a summary is a restatement within a document of the salient findings and conclusions of the document. A summary at the end of a document is intended to complete the orientation of the reader and to present him with the significant ideas to remember, whereas a summary at the beginning of a document is intended to orient the reader in preparation for exploring the entire document, or, perhaps, to place the document and its ideas in context. A summary is different from an abstract in that it assumes that the reader will have the opportunity to peruse the accompanying text. Hence, certain elements essential to a complete understanding of the text, typically the background, purpose and methodology tend not to be present in a summary.

Many other terms are used to denote a regurgitation or abbreviation of document content, some of which can be briefly mentioned. An *abridgement* is usually taken to be a reduction of the original that necessarily omits a number of secondary points, and is, therefore, a relatively general term. A *précis* is an account which restricts itself to the essential points of an argument. A *paraphrase* is an interpretation of the ideas encoded in a document, and a translation into the language of the writer of the paraphrase. A *digest* should be a methodically arranged presentation of the main arguments in a document. And, lastly, a *synopsis* is the term that was originally used to denote a resumé prepared by the author of a work.

The preceding should serve to emphasize some of the different approaches to document abridgement. However, the distinction between one term and another is often not very clear, and the terms are not always used in their strict or any agreed sense.

2.2 The purpose of abstracts

What is the motivation for studying and preparing abstracts? Abstracts are widely used as an aid to the reader in assessing the contents of a document and their potential relevance. The document may be a report, journal article, thesis, patent, contribution in a conference proceedings, standard specification, letter etc. In what respects can a student profit from a knowledge of abstracts and by developing abstracting skills? Plainly, since abstracts are widely used, some librarians and information officers find themselves engaged in preparing abstracts. But even the student who has no intention of entering the sector of the profession that is responsible for the production of abstracts will find abstracting skills valuable. They can help in effective note-taking, digestion of current literature, analysis of committee papers and the presentation of reports. The efficient analysis of professional and technical documents is an asset in many spheres of activity.

Abstracts are a vital aid in document selection and information gathering, and help to avoid duplication and delay in work in progress. In recognition of their importance, abstracts are found in both primary and secondary publications.

Abstracts in primary publications are generally found accompanying reports of research and other developments in both the published and unpublished report literature, in journal articles, reports of professional, scientific and technical meetings and conferences, theses, books and patent applications and specifications. In a journal most formal items including articles, essays, discussions and reviews can be expected to be accompanied by an abstract. Notes, short communications, an article giving a popular treatment and editorials are less likely to carry an abstract. Such abstracts are a valuable indicator of content and facilitate rapid scanning of the contents of documents instead of, or prior to, reading the abstracted document. However, abstracts associated with primary documents are often written by the authors of the documents who are not trained abstractors. These abstracts suffer from the usual limitations of author abstracts (see below).

Abstracts are the cornerstone of secondary publications. Together with indexes, abstracts have for some time constituted a major component of published abstracting services, literature reviews and bibliographies. Today, the large computer-based bibliographic databases also use abstracts as an important means of document representation. Hence, many retrospective and current-awareness services derived from these databases also feature abstracts. Although abstracts have this dual role, they are perhaps more valuable in retrospective searching than in current-awareness devices. The inclusion of abstracts in a current-awareness publication tends to impair the currency of an information service—abstracts take time to prepare. Further, retrospective searches sometimes involve larger numbers of potentially relevant documents than current-awareness scanning, and hence it is more valuable to be able to distinguish between possibly relevant documents rapidly. It is difficult, if not impossible, to scan a large number of complete documents, and it is unlikely that they will all be accessible within one library. Both locally produced abstracts bulletins and other current-awareness services, and abstracts journals feature abstracts. The role of abstracts in these various information tools will be reviewed more fully in Chapter 10.

Wherever abstracts are found they are used for one primary objective: to save the user's time in information gathering and selection. Later, the various types of abstract and their unique roles will be reviewed, but regardless of the type of abstract this objective remains paramount. By digesting information on behalf of the user, and making his information gathering more efficient, the abstractor aims to make a significant impact upon research and decision-making. An improved awareness of existing work should strengthen the foundations of new investigations, and reduce the degree of duplication. An alertness to work in related fields may stimulate creativity in disseminating ideas from one field of study to another, for both the researcher and the manager. In the light of the information explosion, no researcher can now realistically expect to keep pace with developments in his own field, let alone those in allied fields. The expansion of knowledge presents an even more serious problem for other practitioners, such as managers and teachers who need to keep abreast of a relatively wide field in a general way. Abstracts may also make a contribution to overcoming the language barrier, for they make it easier to judge the necessity of translation, and may, on occasions, remove the need for a translation. Abstracts also aid in the compilation and provision of other tools such as indexes, bibliographies and reviews.

Many different abstracts, with different styles and contents, can be derived from one original. Their diversity is related to the extent to which any given abstract is designed to save a user's time, and the diversity of user needs. Although we shall return to this point later, it is convenient now to introduce the idea that the time saved by the abstract for the user depends upon the nature of both the abstract and the original. Some of the factors affecting the value of abstracts are:

(a) *abstract length*: a longer abstract can help in the finer points of selection, but will take longer to write and also longer to scan

(b) *abstract orientation*: an abstract oriented towards a given user's interests will be of maximum value to that user, but will possibly have less utility for other users than an abstract tailored to a general audience

(c) *abstract quality*

(d) *the nature of the original document*: for example, an English-language abstract of a foreign-language document makes some of the ideas in the foreign-language parent document more accessible.

2.3 Types of abstract

There exists a range of labels that are commonly used to describe abstracts. This section examines some of these labels and reviews a variety of approaches to the style and content of an abstract. Despite the school of thought that believes only informative and indicative abstracts can be regarded as true abstracts we will explore many other additional terms. The most appropriate type of abstract in any one set of circumstances will be a function of the nature of the original document and the anticipated readership. For this reason, most information services that have occasion to include abstracts will exploit more than one type of abstract. Further, the labels discussed below are not exclusive, and in some cases it may be appropriate to apply more than one of these labels to one abstract. For example, an abstract may be both informative and homotopic.

Appendixes 2.1 and 2.2 (pp.18-21) provide some examples of the various types of abstracts. The abstracts in Appendix 2.2 are a little artificial since they relate to a part of this book. They have been included so that the reader can compare the abstract with the full text of the document being abstracted. The reader should also examine the abstracts in Figure 1.1.

Informative abstracts present as much as possible of the quantitative or qualitative information contained in a document. This satisfies twin objectives. Informative abstracts both aid in the assessment of document relevance and selection or rejection, and act as a substitute for the document when a superficial or outline knowledge of document content is satisfactory. An informative abstract presents a clear condensation of the essential arguments and findings of the original.

In order to fulfil their twin objectives informative abstracts tend to be lengthier than other abstracts. Typically, papers or journal articles merit abstracts extending to 100 or 250 words, whilst 500 words may be appropriate for more substantial reports and theses. Nevertheless, length should suit the document and an informative abstract need not be of any specified length. Informative abstracts are often easier to write and more desirable than indicative abstracts for texts describing experimental work and documents centred upon one theme, but can be time-consuming and expensive to produce. A fully informative abstract will be impossible to prepare for many discussion papers and reviews, since too many individual and disjointed ideas must be represented. A working rule is to make any abstract as informative as the length of the abstract and the nature of the original permit.

Indicative abstracts are more appropriate representations of discussion and review articles, books and, in some circumstances, conference proceedings, reports without conclusions, essays and bibliographies. An indicative abstract merely indicates the content of an article and contains general statements about the document—no attempt is made to report the actual content of the article as in informative abstracts. Indicative abstracts abound in phrases such as 'is discussed' or 'has been investigated', yet do not record the outcome of the discussions or investigations. Thus, an indicative abstract is no more than a sophisticated selection aid. Since the treatment is more superficial than in an informative abstract, the indicative abstract can be written quickly and economically and requires less perception and subject expertise on the part of the abstractor than an informative abstract. An indicative abstract is not intended to act as a document substitute in the true sense, so its application and value are more limited than those of an informative abstract, and, cost considerations aside, an informative abstract is to be preferred in most instances.

Indicative-informative abstracts are more common than either the pure indicative or the pure informative abstract. Parts of the abstracts are written in the informative style, whilst those aspects of the document that are of minor significance are treated indicatively. When used to good effect this mixed style can achieve the maximum transmission of information, within the minimum length.

Critical abstracts are unusual but have some attractions for the user. A well-produced critical abstract not only describes the document content, but also evaluates the work and its presentation. A critical abstract normally indicates the depth and extent of the work, commenting on the adequacy of experimentation and survey methodology, the assumed background of the intended audience, and the significance of the contribution to the development of knowledge. Critical abstracts are especially effective in pinpointing documents of exceptional interest. However, critical abstracts are rare. Most commercial abstracting services rely upon the refereeing procedure applied to the original document in order to eliminate insignificant and inaccurate submissions. The preparation of a critical abstract not only requires first class abstracting skills but also a subject knowledge which extends beyond a mere understanding, to a full appreciation of the relative significance of various contributions. The abstractor injects his opinions and analysis. Such abstractors are rare, and their time is likely to be expensive.

There are a number of types of very brief abstracts, which, for convenience, will be treated under the term *mini-abstracts*. Mini-abstracts do little more than amplify the title. A good title is already a fair indicator of content (see the sections in Chapter 7 on title indexes, for example) and a number of bibliographical tools and current-awareness services rely upon titles as notification devices, with only occasional supplementary information. A listing of titles is very quick to compile. Equally, because they involve only a little analysis, mini-abstracts are quick to prepare and are particularly important where currency is paramount or abstracting time is at a premium. However, their abridged style presents problems with foreign-language material, and for users whose native language is different from that of the information service. *Short abstracts* comprising only one or two sentences, for instance, may be valuable in commercial information services, or local government news-sheets of the type produced by public libraries. *Telegraphic abstracts* present information exceptionally concisely by resorting to note form. Written in a 'telegram' style, telegraphic abstracts stretch the skills of the abstractor in writing in an abbreviated yet unambiguous style. Some telegraphic abstracts are written in a very standardized format. Such abstracts, sometimes termed 'ruly abstracts' can be viewed as an economical input to a computer-search system. *Keywords* or indexing terms, listed together with a bibliographic citation, may serve as a crude indicator of subject scope.

Slanted abstracts may be informative, indicative, critical or mini-abstracts that have been oriented towards the interests of a known audience. Such abstracts are particularly attractive to the audience for whom they have been drafted, and are therefore often incorporated into in-house abstracting bulletins. For instance, an information unit established to serve the personnel of a food-processing company will seek any reference to food processing, however slight, in the documents that come to the attention of the information staff. Even where food processing only features as a minor aspect of the document content or as a side issue, an abstract slanted towards the audience of the unit might dwell almost entirely upon the information concerning food processing. Slanted abstracts are closely related to *mission-oriented abstracts*. A mission-oriented abstract is an abstract which is prepared for a mission-oriented abstracting service, or an abstracting service that has been charged to cater for the application of a specific branch of knowledge. Another close relation is the *findings-oriented abstract*. These abstracts are slanted or oriented, but in a special sense. They emphasize the results or findings of an investigation, rather than selecting material according to the interests of a given audience. Of particular value to management, and others requiring a rapid overview, findings-oriented abstracts usually start with 'findings' and only later in the abstract return to complete the picture by indicating objectives and methodology. Remember that a conventional abstract adheres as closely as possible to the order of the ideas presented in the original document.

Highlight abstracts are designed to attract the reader's attention to an article and to whet the appetite. Highlight abstracts feature in some primary journals, either as captions preceding the article to which they pertain, or as a supplement to or an expansion of the contents list. No pretence is made of their being either a balanced or complete picture of the article. Indeed, to spark readers' curiosity incomplete and leading remarks are possibly the most effective. In that a highlight abstract cannot stand independent of its associated article it is not a true abstract. Figure 2.1 provides some examples of highlight abstracts.

Fig. 2.1 Examples of highlight abstracts

FEATURES

PLANNING	**Simulation – fast and safe system testing** Most machines in an up-to-date manufacturing environment are linked physically, or by computers or production schedules. But such interdependence can lead to complex systems which need to be organised. Computer simulation is the tool for this **34**
PRODUCTION	**Punch presses – cutting through the sales blurb** This guide to punch press selection examines the advantages/disadvantages of available machine designs, and stresses how workpiece size and shape is critical to every purchase plan **21**
	Exhibitions – a glimpse of what is on the horizon We report on an exhibition in America that 'points the way to new realities, new perceptions and new directions' for one US-based machine tool builder **40**
	CAD/CAM – new system foils long lead times The combination of a computer-aided design and manufacturing (CAD/CAM) system with CNC vertical milling has brought enormous lead times savings at a company that produces aluminium foil containers **51**
MANUFACTURING SUPPORT	**Production control – keeping one step ahead of the rest** A firm in Scotland every year spends £750 000 on new plant. But a computerised production control and data collections system is of equal importance in its quest to stay one step ahead of the competition **56**

Reproduced with permission from *Machinery and production engineering*, 4 February 1987.

Statistical, tabular and numerical abstracts are a means of summarizing numerical data. For this type of data, which may be presented in their original format in a tabular form, a table or other similar device may be the most successful means of summarizing the data. Skill is involved in selecting significant data from the original table or graphical presentation, and drafting a table containing the vital statistics in a more condensed format. Statistical and other numerical abstracts convey effectively certain types of economic, social and marketing data.

Author abstracts or synopses pose a dilemma. They are to be found in any of the earlier mentioned styles or forms. Author abstracts are the abstracts prepared by authors of the document that has been subjected to abstracting. An alternative term is *homotopic abstracts*, literally, published at the same time as the original. Although the two terms homotopic and author abstracts are not synonymous, a large proportion of homotopic abstracts are also author abstracts, so these two concepts will be discussed simultaneously. To what extent can such extracts form the basis for the abstracts which will feature in current-awareness and abstracting services? Theoretically, an author is in a good position to write a sympathetic abstract, and it should be a simple matter to modify the author's abstract to suit the information service. Abstracts are, it must be noted, covered by copyright provisions, and an author may resist direct copying of his abstract. Most abstracting services rely on the fact that it is not generally in the author's interest to restrict copying of abstracts, when their reproduction will draw attention to his original. Other problems associated with the use of author abstracts derive from their nature. Author abstracts can be variable in quality. Some are poorly written giving either too much or too little data, and giving undue emphasis to the author's priorities. Also an author abstract is extremely unlikely to be tailored specifically to the interests of an abstracting organization's clientele. The most satisfactory solution is to use an author abstract as a model, but to submit any author abstracts to thorough editing and checking.

This chapter has now examined a variety of different types of abstract, and Chapter 3 will proceed to introduce methods for the preparation of abstracts.

Appendix 2.1 Examples of types of abstracts
J Rowley, D Butcher and C Turner, 'Consumer information and advice: the role of public libraries', *Aslib proceedings* **32** (11/12), December 1980, 417-24.

Informative abstract
An examination of the work of Consumer Advice Centres and of the information sources and support activities that public libraries can offer. CACs have dealt with pre-shopping advice, education on consumers' rights

and complaints about goods and services, advising the client and often obtaining expert assessments. They have drawn on a wide range of information sources including case records, trade literature, contact files and external links. The recent closure of many CACs has seriously affected the availability of consumer information and advice. Public libraries can make many kinds of information sources more widely available, both to the public and to the agencies now supplying consumer information and advice. Libraries can cooperate closely with advice agencies through local coordinating committees, shared premises, joint publicity, referral and the sharing of professional expertise.

Indicative abstract
The work of Consumer Advice Centres is examined. The information sources used to support this work are reviewed. The recent closure of many CACs has seriously affected the availability of consumer information and advice. The contribution that public libraries can make in enhancing the availability of consumer information and advice both to the public and other agencies involved in consumer information and advice, is discussed.

Extract
With the closure of many CACs, public libraries will need to reassess their existing provision of consumer information sources, and their cooperation with, and support for, the remaining consumer information and advice services in the community.

Indicative-informative abstract
The work of Consumer Advice Centres and the information sources used to support this work are reviewed. The recent closure of many CACs has seriously affected the availability of consumer information and advice. Public libraries can make many kinds of information sources more widely available, both to the public and to the agencies now supplying consumer information and advice. Libraries can cooperate closely with advice agencies through local coordinating committees, shared premises, joint publicity, referral and the sharing of professional expertise.

Short abstract
An examination of the work of Consumer Advice Centres and of the information sources and support activities that public libraries can offer in the field of consumer information and advice.

Keywords
Consumer information; Consumer Advice Centres; Information sources; Advice agencies; Public libraries; Local coordinating committees.

Appendix 2.2 Further examples of types of abstracts

PRECIS indexing system
In: Abstracting and indexing/Jennifer E. Rowley—2nd edition—London: Bingley, 1988—pp.134-149.

Informative abstract

The PRECIS indexing system is a set of procedures for generating pre-coordinate index entries in printed indexes. In PRECIS or PREserved Context Indexing System, each entry presents a précis of the subject content of a document and displays the index terms in context. PRECIS index entries are generated by computer from an indexing string. The string codifies syntactic relationships, establishes a citation order and triggers the generation of references for semantic relationships. Each concept in a string is coded with one of PRECIS's operators, which identifies the role of the concept in the subject description and determines the order of concepts in the string. The role operators are converted into computer instruction codes so that the computer can generate index entries. Index entries are generated under each term designated a lead term. See and See also references are also generated for each concept in the string as necessary. PRECIS was designed for use in the printed index of the *British national bibliography*, but has been used for a number of other printed indexes, and PRECIS strings may be searched with online information retrieval systems.

Indicative abstract

The PRECIS indexing system; a set of procedures for generating pre-coordinate index entries in printed indexes is introduced. The development and applications of PRECIS indexing are outlined. The basic structure of PRECIS indexing strings, the application of operators and the procedures for generating indexing entries are explained with the aid of examples. Semantic relationships and the thesaural aspects of the system are examined, and the value of PRECIS index strings in online searching is considered.

Extract

PRECIS is an alphabetical subject indexing system that both presents a 'précis' of the subject content of a document at each entry point, and also displays index terms in context. The index user can enter the index via any of the concepts present in the compound subject, and locate, at that entry point, the full description of the subject. Each index entry has both a lead term and terms conveying context which are displayed in a way that maximizes the information conveyed by the entry. It must be emphasized that PRECIS is a set of procedures for generating index entries and not an indexing language.

20

Short abstract
PRECIS indexing is a set of procedures for generating index entries in printed indexes. Each entry presents a 'précis' of the subject content of a document, and displays the index terms in context.

Keywords
PRECIS; Indexing systems; Classification theory; Computerized information retrieval; Printed indexes; *British national bibliography.*

Chapter 3

ABSTRACTING

Abstracting is the process of abstraction. Here we use the term in a specialist sense to refer to the preparation of abstracts of the various types discussed in Chapter 2. This chapter introduces some of the principles important to the preparation of a good abstract. However, these guidelines will be of little value and have limited impact unless the reader also attempts some abstracting. Practical application of these ideas, preferably with editorial or tutorial assistance, is the next step after perusing this chapter. Abstracting benefits from a special writing style which improves with practice and training, although those with a naturally concise writing style and an affinity for language may find themselves at an advantage in learning to abstract.

3.1 Selection of documents for abstracting

Before an abstracting programme for any purpose can be initiated, criteria must be established to aid in the identification and selection of documents for which abstracts are to be written. An organization engaged in the preparation of abstracts for some information tool cannot realistically hope to compile an abstract for every document that is pertinent to the topic that it aims to cover. Indeed, in general, it would not be worthwhile to attempt to do so. Seven pointers follow which are useful for discriminating between documents to be abstracted and those not worth abstracting. Different organizations can be expected to accord different significance levels to each of the criteria. Documents that are worthy of consideration for abstracting are:

(a) pertinent to the interests of clients
(b) novel contributions to a given field of endeavour
(c) final reports, or other reports well supported by sound methodology and convincing evidence
(d) those which convey information that is likely to be difficult to access, such as foreign documents or internal reports and memoranda and other documents with a limited circulation
(e) significant advances and reviews
(f) those which contain information located in sources known to be

reliable, such as the information in professional and technical journals with an established reputation

(g) sources, in particular journals or reports issued by a specific organization, for which the abstracting agency has undertaken to give comprehensive coverage.

The selection of documents for abstracting must be closely allied with the proposed application of the abstract and the information that it conveys. Use-based selection policies which are related to the frequency with which documents from various sources or languages are requested by users of the abstracting service have been investigated. Use-based selection policies represent a sound principle, but their implementation depends upon a more effective feedback from user to abstractor than most abstracting agencies can achieve.

3.2 The abstractor

Abstractors come in many guises. The person engaged as an abstractor may be anyone from the author of a work, an information officer, a specialist abstractor or a subject expert to a library assistant or clerk. In some senses an author is in an ideal position to evaluate and summarize his own work, but the fact that he is untrained in abstracting will lead to variations in quality. Some authors make good and others poor abstractors. In choosing abstractors much depends upon the nature of the organization and its resources, as well as upon the purpose of the final abstract. The ideal abstractor is a person with subject expertise, foreign-language abilities and abstracting and information skills. The extent to which each of these facets contributes towards a good abstract is a function of the style and type of abstract and the documents being abstracted. For example, a field where significant advances can be expected to appear regularly in Japanese demands a working familiarity with the Japanese language. Also, informative abstracts make greater demands upon appreciation of subject content than indicative abstracts. Often an abstracting agency must settle for less than the ideal in appointing abstractors. Personnel with the full range of capabilities of value in abstracting are not always available and when they are available may prove expensive.

The larger abstracting organizations train their own abstractors. Volunteer or freelance abstractors may be drawn from the specialists working in academic institutions and trained in abstracting. The chief drawback with volunteer abstractors is the difficulty of controlling the work flow and the return of abstracts. Abstracting may not always be accorded a high priority by volunteer abstractors and undesirable delays may creep into the preparation of abstracts. Scientists, engineers and other subject specialists may be employed together with information scientists as full-time abstractors. Organizations within which abstracting is a relatively minor activity often expect an information officer or librarian to prepare such abstracts as are necessary, in addition to performing various other information duties. In such organizations the librarian or information officer may be called upon not merely to prepare abstracts but also to edit the work of other staff. Abstracts may be submitted for editing and inclusion in bibliographies and bulletins by other information staff and by staff engaged in other activities within the organization, such as research. The consolidation of abstracts into a polished bulletin or list is usually the responsibility of information staff. Most organizations will enlist the services of freelance abstractors with special skills, from time to time. Capabilities with foreign languages, for instance, might usefully supplement the skills of staff abstractors.

3.3 Abstracting procedure

A trainee abstractor will profit from a sequence of distinct steps to aid him in the preparation of an abstract. A four-point plan for abstracting is outlined below. This plan recommends a procedure similar to that used in compiling a précis. More experienced abstractors do not usually adhere to this step-by-step approach; some of the steps merge into each other, or may be conducted simultaneously.

Step 1 Read the document with a view to gaining an understanding of its content and an appreciation of its scope. It may be necessary to read some documents more than once before a satisfactory grasp of their content is achieved. A practised abstractor does not 'read' every word in a document, but scans a significant proportion of the document. Often, but, it must be emphasized, not always, much of the significant information can be culled from the latter paragraphs of a document. Paragraphs headed 'results', 'conclusions', 'recommendations', 'discussion', 'future work' are often fruitful sources of material for inclusion in an abstract. Introductory paragraphs, on the other hand, are generally intended to offer orientation, and may prove particularly helpful to an abstractor with no special knowledge or understanding of the subject of the document. It is important not to let the early sections figure disproportionately in the final abstract merely because they are encountered first.

Step 2 Make written notes of the main points made in the document. Steps 1 and 2 may be completed simultaneously, or Step 2 may be conducted during a re-reading of the document.

Step 3 Draft a rough abstract from notes recorded in Step 2. It is important not to transfer verbose words or phrases from the original and to heed the other points of good style that are summarized in the section below.

Step 4 Check the draft abstract for punctuation, spelling, accuracy,

24

omissions and conciseness. Accuracy is particularly essential. Apart from errors due to general carelessness, proper names and chemical and mathematical formulae are particularly susceptible to mistakes. When all necessary amendments have been spotted, edit the draft abstract and make any improvements to the style that are possible.

Step 5 Write the final abstract.

3.4 Style and content of abstracts

No one style, content or length is appropriate for all abstracts. All three must be tailored to the nature of the original document, the anticipated use of the abstract, and the resources of the abstracting agency. The first set of factors that need to be considered relate to the nature of the original document. Some of the more prominent of these might be:

- length and scope of original document
- subject of original document
- language of original document
- availability of original document
- author's style and emphasis.

Other factors that influence the decision as to preferred length, style and content stem from the anticipated use of the abstract and the requirements of its users. Two points are paramount:

(a) client needs and preferences concerning relatively briefer or longer abstracts may depend upon the field of work or the ease of access to originals or to library and information services.

(b) abstracts planned primarily as alerting devices may be shorter (typically 80 to 100 words) than those abstracts which are to be stored for permanent reference, where 400 to 500 words might, on occasions, be justified.

Lastly, the style, length and contents of an abstract should and will be coloured by the resources of the abstracting agency. Factors here may be:

(a) characteristics of the abstracting staff, such as their proficiency as abstractors, subject knowledge, and other duties demanding their time and attention

(b) total budget available for the production of abstracts. Budgetary considerations are likely to be a factor in determining the amount of abstracting time that can be purchased, or the number of abstractors to be employed

(c) any guidelines set internally, by external agencies or networks restricting the length and content of abstracts, and prescribing stylistic features

(d) the demands of computer processing and/or indexing.

Each abstracting organization must consider many factors before settling upon a specific abstracting format and style. Organizations employing a large team of abstractors will normally abide by a set of abstracting guidelines which impose some standardization with respect to style and content. Smaller organizations may also recognize certain standards, but may not necessarily have any formal written guidelines. However, there are some features of abstracting style and approach that are good practice irrespective of circumstances. Some points which recur in the practices of many abstractors are recorded below.

Points of style and content
Any guidance concerning style and content must be elastic enough to permit the abstractor to use his discretion to achieve a good abstract. One of the main tasks in writing a successful abstract is to convey the maximum quantity of information using the minimum number of words. The objective is to summarize the contribution made by the original's author, including why the work was done, what conclusions were reached and how they arose, but to exclude any peripheral material. Brevity is all-important. It both saves the reader's time and lowers the cost of disseminating the abstract. Many devices that are accepted as good style in other types of writing, and indeed serve a useful function, must be avoided in abstracting. In pursuing brevity, however, care must be exercised to avoid ambiguity.

1 An abstract often starts with a 'topic' or 'lead' sentence. This first sentence attempts to summarize any essential information that is not conveyed by the title. The objective is to enable the reader to eliminate possibly relevant documents, which, in fact, prove to be of little interest without delving into the body of the abstract. Hence, any elements that might contribute to relevance assessment must be incorporated into the topic sentence. These facts or ideas, like any that are introduced elsewhere, do not need to be repeated in the remaining abstract text.

2 The abstractor must resist the temptation to use long sentences in striving to avoid repetition. Flow and readability should not be sacrificed to brevity. Sentences with an average length in the region of 12 words are likely to yield a readable abstract.

3 All abstracts, barring possibly those of exceptional length, should consist of one paragraph only. This should be a coherent paragraph, and not a series of disjointed sentences. Only the first line need not be a proper sentence, and might read, for example: 'Points to forecasting's relationship with planning and. . .' All sentences should be complete, and verbs, prepositions and articles should not be omitted. A style that provides continuity should be adopted, even if this is contrary to normal language

usage. Separate paragraphs may be introduced for long documents such as theses, reports etc, where different topics are introduced.

4   A device which is acceptable and widely used in abstracts is to number and list points within a sentence. This is particularly appropriate in indicative abstracts.

5   Ambiguous words, and terms whose meaning is otherwise unclear, should be avoided. Ambiguity depends upon the background of the readers, but abbreviations, acronyms, trade names and subject jargon are all potentially confusing. Such terms contribute to brevity and ought to be used to maximum effect, but they must be used with care if comprehensibility is to be maintained. Some abbreviations are well known to many audiences. For example, °C, cm and kg may safely be introduced as necessary. Other abbreviations are familiar to specialist audiences and may happily be used under such circumstances, but need to be explained for the benefit of a general audience. For example, in psychology, S for subject, and E for experimenter are common parlance. A chemist would recognize 'wt' for weight, 'ppt' for precipitate, and 'DC' for direct current. Acronyms and other abbreviations may be safely used if on their first appearance they are explained or written in their expanded form, alongside the abbreviation, e.g. 'British Broadcasting Corporation (BBC)' or 'temporary threshold shift (TTS)'. Many abstracting organizations abide by a standard list of abbreviations. This list may be published in their abstracting product at intervals.

6   Conciseness is paramount. Redundant phrases such as: 'the authors studied', 'in this work', 'the paper concludes by', 'this can be taken to indicate that', 'these discussions lead to the recommendations that', should be avoided if at all possible. Equally, all verbose phrases and clauses should be supplanted by a more concise form. Never use a clause where a briefer phrase will do, or a phrase where one word will suffice. Thus:

- 'Ss in this study were' is replaced by 'Ss were'
- 'in order to' is replaced by 'to'
- 'in a similar fashion' is replaced by 'similarly'
- 'it would seem that' is replaced by 'seemingly'
- 'was considered to be' is replaced by 'was'
- 'has been found to increase' is replaced by 'increased'.

Active verbs allow concise and direct expression. A simple past tense describes more effectively what was done and the present tense may be used in dealing with facts, properties etc, which still hold true. Remember, however, that clarity is as vital as brevity.

7   Style and order of ideas should mirror that of the author, unless there are sound grounds for modification.

We have noted a number of central features of a good abstracting style. What of content? In this the abstract must reflect the original document.

The next section develops this theme. In selecting content it is important to remember that the abstractor is expected to reflect the authors' emphases, priorities, order and language as far as is reasonable. Unless a conscious decision has been made to the contrary, the abstractor should not introduce any new biases or emphases.

Many of the documents for which abstracts must be prepared are research papers, reports or journal articles. The abstracts of research papers will typically have each of the following aspects of the original research document represented:

(a) the purpose and scope of the investigation—this will help in relevance assessment, especially if the type of treatment, e.g. experimental, theoretical, is specified
(b) the methodology employed, in particular, apparatus, equipment, tools, materials
(c) the results obtained
(d) the conclusions drawn
(e) incidental findings (e.g. properties, side-effects, important inconsistencies in arguments or deductions, newly discovered data sources). Anything that is common knowledge to those conversant with the field should be omitted. History or background, descriptions of well-known techniques, equipment, processes, conclusions, axioms and results need not be incorporated into an abstract. The abstract should concentrate on new terms, theories, hypotheses, results and conclusions. Abstracts should be precise and distinguish clearly between conjecture and established fact. Numerical data should be accurately reiterated together with any margin of error. Standard tests, techniques and apparatus should be referred to by their full names.

3.5 Abstracts of special types of documents

The guidelines presented so far are admirable for abstracts of journal articles and research papers, but special considerations must be introduced for various types of documents. A few of the more essential of these are reviewed here.

Reviews and surveys both demand an indicative abstract, which defines the limits of the subject area under review, and the depth of the treatment. A general paper may be irrelevant to a specialist but of genuine value to someone seeking a brief introduction to a field peripheral to their main interest. A review, as opposed to a survey, should be a critical, liberally documented assessment of work in a particular field, and is usually supported by an extensive bibliography. A review author can be expected to comment on:

- the purpose of the review
- the sources used to support the content
- the conclusions drawn from the content.

An abstract of a review should attempt to reflect all of these aspects. An indication of the exhaustiveness and currency of a review can be gleaned from an examination of the bibliography.

Bibliographies merit an indicative abstract. Significant bibliographies are invaluable tools and it is important that their appearance be acknowledged. An abstract of a bibliography can be expected to note:

- the kind of annotations or abstracts supplied
- whether author affiliations are given
- language
- the arrangement of the bibliography (e.g. subject or author)
- the existence of indexes
- the subject scope of the bibliography
- the sources of the literature included
- the period covered
- the intended audience.

Monographs and conference proceedings may be treated in their entirety, or, if they comprise a series of distinct reviews or contributions, each individual contribution may be abstracted in accordance with its unique nature and content. When such documents are treated in their entirety by one abstract an indicative abstract will be found to suit a monograph or conference proceedings. An indication of scope should be given, and the level of the audience noted. The table of contents, in a condensed form, is often used as a means of describing scope and contents. The indicative abstract of the complete publications may be supplemented or supplanted by informative abstracts of the individual contributions.

Patents abstracting is a special skill, involving not only a technical knowledge, but also a facility for unravelling the special legalistic jargon in which patents abound. The patent abstract is a concise statement of the technical disclosure of the patent and must emphasize that which is new in the context of the invention. Abstracting organizations tend to be interested primarily in the technical and not the legal content of a patent. Patents are one of the first sources of many technical developments. Typically a patent abstract is informative, and includes:

- in the case of a machine or apparatus, its organization and operation
- in the case of an article, its method of making or manufacture
- in the case of a chemical compound, its identity and use
- in the case of a mixture, its ingredients
- in the case of a process, the steps, the type of reaction, conditions etc.

Short communications, newspaper articles and letters to the editor present problems in abstracting, both from the selection viewpoint and also as to abstract content. Such contributions are often already compressed and may in themselves be shorter than a standard-length abstract. Abstracts of such articles should concentrate upon adding precise information concerning the issue under discussion to the information conveyed by the title. Short abstracts are generally preferred, but there are instances where the most effective approach is to cite the original unamended, and to state that this is what has been done.

3.6 Abstracting guidelines

Many organizations engaged in the preparation of abstracts compile a set of instructions for abstractors. Guidelines are particularly necessary when abstracting is being conducted by abstractors in physically distinct units. This may arise under the following circumstances:

- an international abstracting organization with several national agencies inputting material
- an abstracting organization reliant upon volunteer abstractors who are scattered across national boundaries
- an abstracting organization making use of freelance abstractors. Guidelines are also valuable introductory material for any new abstractors, whether geographically separated from the remainder of the abstracting team or not. They can also convey complex instructions concerning the formatting and organization necessary for computer inputting. Some examples of guidelines are listed in the reading list on p.172. Guidelines can be expected to discuss some or all of the following:

(a) instructions on the way in which abstracts are to be presented, e.g. typing, paper, layout, spacing
(b) style and length of abstracts
(c) language of the abstract and the treatment of foreign-language materials
(d) abstracting procedures (how to go about the preparation of abstracts)
(e) special approaches to abstracting for various types of material
(f) form of bibliographic reference or citation
(g) lists of standard abbreviations, including those of journal titles and standard forms of quoting chemical nomenclature and mathematical expressions
(h) introduction to the abstracting service and an explanation of the nature and use of abstracts
(i) indexing instructions, especially if the abstractor and indexer are one and the same person. These instructions may include index terms and classified headings or notation

(j)   sample forms for completing and submitting abstracts, including instructions for conformity with computer processing

(k)   examples of abstracts in various fields of interest to the abstracting organization

(l)   the criteria to be used in selecting items for abstracting, e.g. subject, form, source

(m)   transliteration and the practices to be adopted when citing items in languages with non-Roman alphabets

(n)   proofreading procedures and marks.

ISO 214 *Documentation-abstracts for publication and documentation.* Geneva, ISO, 1976, provides a useful outline on the basic principles of writing informative abstracts, and is used by some abstracting agencies as a substitute for an in-house manual.

3.7   Abstracting and computerized information-retrieval systems

Many of the abstracts written today are put into computerized information-retrieval systems and become an important component of computerized databases. Abstracts written for inclusion in secondary services are often put immediately into a database. Abstracts written by authors for inclusion in primary journals may appear in printed form, and then later be recorded in a database as a representation of the document with which they are associated. The style and content of the abstract should not be affected by its storage in a computer database. The computer is merely a store. The abstracts are still used to summarize the literature of a subject field, although the ways in which they are used may become more numerous. It remains important that the abstract be an accurate representation of the content of the document, and that the abstract be easy for the reader to scan and digest.

There is, however, one major factor to be considered in abstract style and content when abstracts are included in a database. The words in abstracts in a database are often used in the free-text searching of that database. The abstract thus becomes an important retrieval tool.

Fidel has examined the effect that this has had on abstracting policies. Editors consider content of abstracts and their languages as a primary factor in retrieval enhancement. Most recommend that once abstractors have decided which concepts to include in abstracts and in which form to represent them, their terms should be coordinated with index terms assigned from a controlled vocabulary. It is suggested that editors have developed abstracting policies from their own experience of free-text searching, rather than from any research results. A short list of the guidelines for writing abstracts that were identified by Fidel's study is given in Appendix 3.1. Clearly, further investigations in this area are important for a future which heralds not only electronic secondary publications, but also electronic primary publications.

Appendix 3.1   Some guidelines on the content of abstracts for use in free-text searching

The content of abstracts

General statements
Use 'important' concepts and terms (e.g. those which will enhance free-text retrieval, those for which a document gives enough information, or key words).

Index terms
Co-ordinate concepts used in abstracts with assigned descriptors.

(a)   Assign concepts in abstracts that are identical to descriptors.
(b)   Assign concepts in abstracts that complement descriptors (e.g. relevant terms that are missed in descriptor indexing and in titles, terms that are more specific than descriptors, or a particular type of term that is important to the subject area, such as geographic names).
(c)   Assign concepts in abstracts that both complement and are identical to descriptors.

Enhance indexing independent of any index language used.

Check lists
Follow a list of retrieval-related elements that should be included in abstracts.
Forms of check lists:

(a)   Categories that should be included in abstracts (e.g. materials, properties and processes) and the conditions under which they should be included (e.g. only when they are discussed elaborately, or whenever mentioned).
(b)   Specific and particular guidelines (e.g. 'whenever dealing with a new product, mention the company name').

The language of abstracts

Use of author language
Use author language.
Do not use author language.

(a)   Use standardized and concrete terms specific to a subject area.

Use both author language and synonyms.

Relationship to index language used
Co-ordinate terms in abstracts with descriptors.
Complement descriptors with terms in abstracts (e.g. use synonyms or more specific terms).
Use specific and well-accepted terms for particular categories (such as materials, processes and products).

Practices to avoid
Do not use the negative (e.g. use *sick* instead of *not healthy*).
Do not list terms which have a common last word as a series (such as 'upper, middle, and working class').

Word forms
Follow local language practices (e.g. change American spelling for British databases).
Always spell out terms in certain categories (such as processes, materials, products).
When a term and a descriptor are the same, record the term in the form used by the descriptor.
Express terms both in their abbreviated form and in their complete form.

Reproduced with permission from Fidel, R., 'Writing abstracts for free-text searching', *Journal of documentation*, **42** (1), March 1986, 11-21.

Chapter 4

BIBLIOGRAPHIC REFERENCES

4.1 Citation principles

All abstracts must be accompanied by an adequate bibliographic reference in any publications or other applications where they appear remote from the parent document. In most applications abstracts are announcement media—without the possibility of referral to the original document severe limitations are imposed upon the value of the abstract. In order to fulfil this function satisfactorily, references must be accurate and adhere to some set of rules or standards. The precise contents of a reference and its format are decisions to be made by the individual abstracting organization, although, despite wide variations in practice between the standards adopted by the various abstracting agencies, certain elements are generally considered vital. The examples given later demonstrate the diversity of citation practices in abstracting and indexing publications. In the interests of consistency, and in order to introduce the possibility of matching entries in different databases, it is preferable that document citations are in line with some internationally accepted standard. Some types of materials may be cited in accordance with various internationally recognized codes and standards. Amongst these standards are those embodied in the International Standard Bibliographic Description programme and those enumerated in cataloguing codes such as the Anglo-American Cataloguing Rules, and their equivalents in other languages. Although these standards have been drafted with the primary objective of describing documents in a suitable manner for listings in catalogues and bibliographies, they may also be acceptable to some extent as the basis of citation practices in abstracting publications. Such standards are concerned to describe documents as bibliographic units, and are helpful for citing complete works such as monographs, reports, official publications and conference proceedings, but their recommendations concerning parts of publications leave something to be desired. Guidelines for journal articles, or individual contributions in conference proceedings, are not always appropriate or sufficiently concise. Here, other standards that have been framed explicitly in relation to the citation of such materials should be more effective.

In the light of the widely varying practices that are to be found in abstracting and indexing publications it is difficult to make any precise comments concerning bibliographic citation practices. This chapter attempts to raise some of the issues that are common to any citation standard, and to reflect current international standards. The following are preliminary issues that must be decided in all cases.

1 The primary source of data for the bibliographic citation of print material is usually the title page or other appropriate parts of the work. For non-print materials data must be drawn from the work, its container or accompanying printed material.

2 Elements to be included will vary according to the type of material concerned and this issue will be developed later. There is also the question of how much detail should be recorded. The most abbreviated form conveys only the minimum amount of information necessary to identify the work uniquely. Beyond this various other levels of detail may be included either to convey something of the nature or content of a work, or to facilitate the identification of a work.

3 Organization of the elements of the bibliographic citation will be considered later in respect of individual materials.

4 As regards punctuation and capitalization, various practices are adopted under different circumstances. It is important that punctuation and capitalization contribute to the legibility and/or comprehension of the citation.

5 As regards abbreviations, and the extent to which they are used, most citation standards subscribe to the use of abbreviations. It is preferable to take account of international standards where these are available, e.g. standards for the abbreviation of periodical titles.

4.2 Periodical article citation

This discussion of citation practices in abstracting publications commences with periodical article citation. Periodical articles occur very commonly in abstracting publications and databases, and so abstracting agencies' citation recommendations may be preoccupied with the practices desirable for periodical articles.

The components of a full citation for a periodical article (in addition to an abstract) will normally be:

- document identification number
- author(s)
- title
- source reference, including periodical title, date of issue, volume number, issue number and pagination.

Sometimes the following additional data are also present:

- sponsoring agency, and its report number
- contract number

- original language and/or source of a translation
- any other additional descriptive notes.

There is no established order for these components. Title may precede author, or vice versa. It is important for the citation to be formatted so as to facilitate scanning; this usually means making the title easy to spot and extract from the remainder of the text on the page. This may either be achieved by appropriate type face, or by the positioning of the title. A title is frequently the first element in a citation.

For articles in periodicals there are a number of International Standards Organization standards which provide guidance. ISO 690-1975 *Document-ation–Bibliographical references–Essential and supplementary elements* gives some suggestions concerning the structure of a bibliographic reference for periodical articles. The parallel BS 1629:1976 *Recommend-ations for bibliographical references* provides guidance for the presentation of references to books and other separately issued publications, serials, contributions, articles and patents.

Further comments on each of the first four components of the citation follow. The *document identification number* is a number which provides the unique identification of the document in the abstracting publication or other related product in which the document is announced. The number is usually a sequential number assigned to a document record on admission to a database or printed product.

Author name(s) provide rapid identification of an article. They may be entered in an author index, or merely used as an additional filing element within a sequence of entries basically arranged by subject. Various practices for recording names persist, despite the advantages to be gained by standardization. There are many circumstances in which it would be desirable to be able to match the entries on different databases. The author name(s) must form a primary key in the matching process, and common practices would make matching much easier. Cataloguing codes such as the Anglo-American Cataloguing Rules provide some systematic and workable guidelines on the citation of the authors' names, which might well be adopted more widely. There are three categories of problem in the citation of author names:

(a) who is responsible for the authorship of the work?
(b) what is the name by which the author should most effectively be described?
(c) in what form should the author's name be presented?

These three areas for decisions lead, in the specific instance of periodical articles, to a number of issues that commonly arise and must be settled in the interests of consistency in citation practices. Some of the more recurrent issues to be considered include the following:

(a) articles with *many authors*: are all names to be cited, or only the first named, or a given number of names (e.g. two or three)? Further, in what order should names be quoted?

(b) articles with only or additionally the name of a *corporate body* associated with them: can a corporate body be accorded authorship responsibility?

(c) bodies and people with *more than one name*: which name should be used?

(d) bodies and people that have names that are or may be *cited in different ways*: typical problem area is whether personal names should be cited in full, or whether only the surname and initials should be given. If initials only are noted effort is saved in reproducing full names and seeking out full forenames where these are not readily evident. However, the more abbreviated form may result in confusion of different authors with the same initials. Another issue is whether names should be inverted, i.e. family name followed by forename, and if inversion is practised how foreign names, prefixed names and double-barrelled names are to be treated. Corporate body names also present problems. Are abbreviated forms acceptable? How much of the name of a parent body is necessary for identification? In which order should individual components be cited? These are but some of the areas of concern.

The examples in Figure 4.1 show the citation practices that are evident in certain printed abstracting and indexing publications. Similar practices are evident in the equivalent databases, and the sample records in Chapter 1 should also be examined.

Fig. 4.1 Some periodical article citations

Electrical and electronics abstracts

53937 Fabrication and characterization of titanium-indiffused proton-exchanged optical waveguides in Y-LiNbO$_3$. A.L.Dawar, S.M.Al-Shukri, R.M.De La Rue, A.C.G.Nutt, G.Stewart (Dept. of Electron. & Electr. Eng., Glasgow Univ., Scotland).
Appl. Opt. (USA), vol.25, no.9, p.1495-9 (1 May 1986). — Abstract

53939 Analysis of errors in regulation of cylindrical step-index optical waveguide fiber with a spherical lens excited with G&As lasers. Zhang Zhipeng, Shi Shouyong (Dept of Phys., Xiamen Univ., China).
Chin. J. Lasers (China, vol.12, no.12, p.729-31, 741 (20 Dec. 1985) in Chinese [received: 20 May 1985] — Abstract

Fig. 4.1 continued

53940 **Locating optical fibre faults.** A.Wiltshire (Cossor Electron., Harlow, England).
Commun. Int. (GB), vol.12, no.1, p.59-60, 65-6 (Jan. 1985). [received: 10 Apr 1985] — Abstract

54350 Cross-polarized radiation of folding umbrella-type mirror antennas. M.V.Gryanik, V.I.Loman, I.K.Nesterenko.
Radioelectron. & Commun. Syst. (USA), vol.28, no.5, p.40-2 (1985). Translation of: *Izv. VUZ Radioelektron. (USSR),* vol.28, no.5, p.43-6 (1985). [received: 12 Jun 1986] — Abstract

Library and information science abstracts

TogsGjFr(61)—On-line. Medical school libraries. UK. Charing Cross and Westminster Medical School. CAIRS (Computer Assisted Information Retrieval System) 86/4736
Using an information retrieval package, CAIRS, as an OPAC in a small, university medical library. Nicky Whitsed. *Program,* 20 (2) Apr 86, 196-203. 8 refs. — Abstract

TsAsD433—Standards for. West Germany 86/4738
Universal-Dokumentationssprache Anspruch und Wirklichkeit aus bibliothekarischer Sicht. [Universal documentation language—claims and reality from a librarian's point of view.] Gisela Hartwieg. *Mitteilungsblatt (Verband der Bibliotheken des Landes Nordrhein-Westfalen).* 35 (3), Sept 85, 274-279. 29 refs. — Abstract

Ueg&Oun—On-line catalogues. Microcomputers 86/4740
Microcomputers and online catalogs. Michael Gorman. *Drexel Library Quarterly,* 20 (4) Fall 84, 25-33. — Abstract

ZmRn&—Data bases. Information services. Front end systems and Gateway facilities. WILSONLINE. WILSEARCH 86/4787
Wilsearch: a new departure for an old institution. Mick O'Leary. *Online,* 10 (2) Mar 86, 102-107, illus. — Abstract

ZmRnM(37)Mg—Data bases. Information services. Education. Audiovisual materials. Law libraries 86/4792
Audiovisual materials and the law librarian. Elizabeth Oliver. *Law Librarian,* 16 (2) Aug 85, 81-83, 1 ref. — Abstract

Engineering index

080702 COMPLIANCE WITH SOLVENT EMISSION REGULATIONS ESSENTIALLY WITHOUT CHANGING RESINS, PIGMENTS OR BASIC EQUIPMENT. — Abstract

Brewer, George E.F. (Coating Consultants, Birmingham, MI, USA). *Plat Surf Finish* v 71 n 5 May 1984 p 97-100.

Fig. 4.1 continued

080704 HOW TO INSTALL A PAINTING ROBOT. — Abstract

Susnjara, Ken (Thermwood Robotics Corp, Dale, IN, USA). *Rob World* v 2 n 7-8 Jul-Aug 1984 p 24-26.

080070 CATALYTIC OXIDATION OF DIMETHYLSULFIDE TO DIMETHYLSULFOXIDE BY OXYGEN IN THE GAS PHASE — Abstract

Mishkina, A.V.; Shepler, V.S.; Meshcheryakov, V.D. *Kinet Catal* v 25 n 6 pt 1 Nov-Dec 1984 p 1187-1190.

072360 FORMATION OF THE STRATABOUND KELLHUANI TIN DEPOSITS. BOLIVIA — Abstract

Lehmann, B. (Mission Geologique Allemande, Bujurobura, Burundi). *Miner Deposita* v 20 n 3 Jul 1985 p 169-176.

The *title* of an article is an important indicator of subject content, and may also function as a filing and identifying element of the citation. In the interests of document identification, the title is normally quoted verbatim so that the document record can be successfully and confidently matched with the document. In special circumstances titles may be modified. Uninformative or unclear titles may be augmented by additional words; these words are usually enclosed in square brackets in order to distinguish them from the authentic title. An abstract may also serve to elucidate an unclear title. Titles of foreign-language publications are generally cited in both the original language and in the translated language. Scanning is facilitated if the translated title appears prior to the original title, but the original title must be retained for successful identification of the original document even if users will not benefit directly from the presence of the title.

The description of the *source* of a periodical article comprises: periodical title, date of issue, volume number, issue number and pagination. The first element, the periodical title, will often appear in an abbreviated form. Standards exist that embody recommendations concerning periodical title abbreviation. ISO 4-1986 *Documentation rules for the abbreviation of title words and titles of publications* presents an international code for the abbreviation of titles of periodicals. Its British equivalent is BS 4148:1985 *Specification for abbreviation of title words and titles of publications*. ISO 832-1975 contributes specifically by listing abbreviations of typical words in bibliographic references. The international list of periodical title word abbreviations is maintained by the International Serials Documentation System (ISDS), International

39

Centre in Paris. Most abstracting organizations work from their own standard list of abbreviations. Although abbreviations avoid the tedium of copying and reading lengthy titles, abbreviations have disadvantages. Some common abbreviations may come to be recognized by most abstractors and users (e.g. 'J.') but many abbreviations will need to be checked in a list of abbreviations. Confusion can arise when different abstracting agencies use the same abbreviation to represent different words. Journal titles will normally be accompanied by an indication of the issue in which the article is contained. Volume and issue or part numbers will provide this information. These may be presented in a variety of ways, either explicitly (e.g. volume 5, number 6) or with the intercession of variations in typeface (e.g. 5 (6)). Volume and part numbers are not essential if other components of the citation are adequate for the identification of the original article. For instance, if the date of the issue uniquely identifies the issue, and/or the pagination is continuous throughout a volume, volume and part numbers may be redundant. Where they are present, the date may follow volume and part numbers, and where they are absent it takes their place. The date of the issue is cited as fully as is necessary to identify the issue and usually in the format specified in the publication. For example, a monthly periodical will be identified by month and year, whilst a weekly serial requires the date in the month, the month and the year. Page numbers are also necessary and may be inserted in various positions. Page numbers should be cited in accordance with the exact pages on which the text of an article appears. Thus, where the text of an article is interspersed amongst advertisements, letters and other contributions, only those pages on which parts of the article are printed are listed. For example, a statement of the following form would indicate all of the pages upon which text is to be found: 3, 4, 6-8, 10. Pagination should be inclusive and show full page numbers. For example, 287-293 is preferred to 287-93 and 331-338 is preferred to 331-8.

Punctuation will be present in the reference and should aid in distinguishing one component from another. As the examples in figure 4.1 show, there is a wide variety of practices concerning punctuating citations. Punctuation is present in order to partition the elements of a citation and should contribute to its comprehension.

4.3 Book and report citation

In most subject areas, especially within science and technology, books are less numerous than periodical articles, and thus the problem of their citation looms less significantly in abstracting and indexing products than that of the citation of periodical articles. If, however, practices are established that are appropriate to both monographs (such as textbooks) and technical and research reports, then these practices can be applied to a not insignificant proportion of the materials covered by abstracting publications.

The primary distinction between the citation of periodical articles and the citation of books and reports lies in the fact that the former are parts of documents whereas the latter are complete documents in their own right. The common feature of citation practices regardless of the material being listed is their variety. Figure 4.2 shows some of the practices that are adopted in the citation of books and reports.

Fig. 4.2 Some book and report citations

Electrical and electronic abstracts

39391 Trend analysis for light water reactor units performance. Availability predictions for Finnish nuclear power units. E. Lehtinen.
Report 382 Trend Res Centre Finland, Electr. Eng. Lab., Espoo (Dec 1985), 99 pp. — Abstract

39389 Risk-based evaluation of technical specifications
Report EPRI-NP-4317. Electr. Power Res. Inst., Palo Alto, CA, USA (31 Dec. 1985). 180 pp. — Abstract

39392 Nuclear unit operating experience: 1983-1984 update.
Report EPRI-NP-4368, Electr. Power Res. Inst., Palo Alto, CA, USA (31 Jan. 1985). 256 pp. — Abstract

39390 Human engineering design guidelines for maintainability.
Report EPRI-NP-4350, Electr. Power Res. Inst., Palo Alto, CA, USA (31 Dec. 1985). 290 pp. — Abstract

39393 Degradation of building materials over a lifespan of 30-100 years.
G.H. Lewis.
Report EUR 10020 EN, Comm. European Communities, Luxembour, (1985), 9-63 pp. Contract DE-A-001-UK. — Abstract

Library and information science abstracts

85/6366

A comparison of *Excerpta Medica* and MEDLINE for the provision of drug information to health care professionals. Bernard Houghton, John Smith, Victoria A.D. Webster, Susan Huey (n p). British Library, Research and Development Department, 1983, 63p, illus, tables, refs. (BLRD report 5834) —Abstract

85/6502

Book, schools and an urban community. A study of the unusual growth of school bookshops in the London Borough of Newham. Anne Crisp, John Eversley, Paul Cockburn, Ray Phillips. London, Newham Parents Centre, 1983, 116p. illus, tables, bibliog. (BLRD report 5833). — Abstract

Fig. 4.2 continued

85/6293

Videotex development in the United States. Michael B. Binder. In *Advances in library administration and organisation, volume 2; edited by G. McCabe and B. Kreissman, Greenwich, Connecticut and London, England, Jai Press, 1983,* 39-68. 7 refs. bibliog. — Abstract

85/6474

BLEND-1 : Background and developments. B. Shackel, D.J. Pullinger. London. British Library, 1984. 152p. illus, tables, refs, bibliog. (Library and Information Research Report 29). (ISBN 0-7123-3042-9). — Abstract

Engineering index

080701 COMPARISON OF TT-F-1098 SOLVENT-THINNED BLOCK FILLERS WITH WATER-THINNABLE BLOCK FILLERS. — Abstract

Johnston, Susan (US Army Construction Engineering Lab, Engineering & Materials Div., Champaign, IL, USA). *Tech Rep US Army Corp Eng Constr Eng Res Lab* M-85-09 Mar 1985 13p.

070060 RETENTION OF ZINC, CADMIUM, COPPER, AND LEAD BY GEOLOGIC MATERIALS. — Abstract

Gibb, James P. (Illinois State Water Survey, Groundwater Section, IL, USA); Cartwright, Keros. *Coop Groundwater Rep Ill State Water Surv Ill State Geol Surv* 9 1982 121p.

The components recognized by the International Standard Bibliographic Description (ISBD) programme as being appropriate for the precise identification of a document represent a recognized approach to document citation. The programme has, to date, established standards for monographs (ISBD(M)), serials (ISBD(S)), maps (ISBD(CM)), music (ISBD (PM)), and non-book materials (ISBD(NBM)). A general framework is prescribed in the ISBD(G), where G stands for General. The components of the ISBD(G) are shown in figure 4.3.

Fig. 4.3   The ISBD(G) framework

Area	Preceding punctuation	Element
Each area is preceded by a stop, space, dash, space (. −).		
1 Title and statement of responsibility area	[ ] = : / ;	A Title proper B *General medium designation* *C Parallel title *D Other title and title information E First statement of responsibility *F Second or subsequent statement of responsibility
2 Edition or issue area	/ ;	A Edition or issue statement B First statement of responsibility relating to the edition *C Second or subsequent statement of responsibility relating to the edition
3 Medium (or type of publication) specific area		
4 Publication, distribution etc. area	 : [ ] ; , (:)	A First place of publication, distribution etc. *B Name of publisher, distributor etc. *C *Statement of function of publisher, distributor etc.* *D Second or subsequent place of publication, distribution etc. *E Date of publication, distribution etc. *F *Place of manufacture* *G *Name of manufacturer*
5 Physical description area	 : ; +	A Specific medium designation B Extent of item C Other physical details D Dimensions of item E *Accompanying material*
6 Series area Each set of information relating to a series is enclosed by parentheses (( ))	= : ; . = : ;	A Series statement *B Parallel series statement C Standard serial numbering of series D Numbering within series E Sub-series statement *F Parallel sub-series statement G Standard serial numbering of sub-series H Numbering within sub-series
7 Notes area		A Note
8 Standard number (or alternative) and terms of availability area	( ) :	A Standard number (or alternative) B *Qualification added to standard number (or alternatives)* C *Terms of availability and/or price*

ISBD(G)—General notes on the framework
—Elements italicized are optional.
—Elements preceded by an asterisk may be repeated when necessary.
—Areas 7 (Notes) and 8 (Standard number etc.) may be repeated when necessary.

Guidance on selection of the pieces of information to be included in each of the areas of the ISBD(M) or ISBD(G) is to be found in cataloguing rules. The framework provided by the ISBD(G) is sufficiently comprehensive to be applicable to all types of media, whilst, at the same time, making it possible to distinguish one work from another, and one edition from another of the same work. The ISBD(M) indicates that the description for monographs should include:

- title and statements of authorship
- edition statement and statements of authorship relating to the edition
- imprint (i.e. place of publication, publisher, date of publication)
- collation (i.e. number of volumes or pagination, illustration statement, size)
- series statement
- notes
- ISBN, binding, price.

The ISBD(M) is merely an explanatory framework. A cataloguing code also touches on the subject of bibliographic description. Cataloguing codes consider in detail the problems that are likely to be encountered in entering parts of the ISBD. Knotty problems such as which of a series of publishers' names and places of publication to record, fall within the ambit of a cataloguing code. The size of the Anglo-American Cataloguing Rules illustrates that there are many problems of this kind, and we cannot attempt to consider them here. Suffice it to say that there are some problems associated with recording all components in the description.

The framework recommended by the ISBD(M) is intended to cater for reports, although an abstracting agency will probably be selective in the components that it includes. The report series title and any report number may be inserted in the series statement area. Other areas may be redundant for report literature. Illustration statements, for example, are unlikely to be necessary.

Many abstracting and indexing publications adopt a much more restricted style of citation than is embodied in the ISBD(M), but, in general, the elements included represent a subset of those comprising an ISBD(M). Elements that are commonly omitted include the place of publication, collation statement, binding and price. The examples in figure 4.2 demonstrate the range of practices in use in some abstracting and indexing publications. These examples serve to introduce a further point. Although the elements to be included in a citation may match those in the ISBD(M), the extent of the detail presented in each area may vary between publications. The author statement may, for example, name all of a string of authors, or just the first named. Multiple publishers may all be acknowledged, or one alone may be represented. Also, variations in the order of components in citations can be expected between different publications. In particular, the author is often cited prior to the title in order that the author's name may function as an alphabetical ordering device.

4.4 The citation of conference proceedings
Conference proceedings are singled out for special attention because they are an important category of material in relation to abstracting and indexing publications, and also their citation poses unique and potentially bewildering problems. Clear and firm guidance is needed to prevent confusion and inconsistencies in the citation of conference proceedings. Two areas of concern may be crystallized: the citation of a volume of conference proceedings, and the citation of one contribution in such a volume.

Once again, for the citation of a volume of conference proceedings the ISBD(M) and the Anglo-American Cataloguing Rules should prove useful allies. But, also yet again, practices concerning the citation of conference proceedings vary. Difficulties arise from the plethora of information presented in many conference proceedings. Particular attention must be paid to:

● names of editors of the proceedings
● title of the conference (possibly distinct from the title of the pro-ceedings)
● title of the series of conferences and the number of the conference within that series (if the conference is one of a series)
● location of the conference
● date of the conference
● names of the agents of organizations acting as sponsors to the con-ference.

This gamut of information presents the indexer and user with problems in choosing access points for conference proceedings. There are a greater variety of potential access points than is normally encountered with monographs; no one body or person can be universally recognized as author. The examples in figure 4.4 show some of the approaches to solving these problems.

The citation of individual articles in conference proceedings is merely a matter of adding the details, e.g. title, author(s) and page numbers, of the individual contribution to a citation of the full volume. The individual contribution is described first, followed by a sufficient description of its location for the volume to be traced.

Fig. 4.4 Some conference proceedings citations

Electrical and electronics abstracts

54353 Inflatable, space-rigidized reflectors for mobile missions.
M.C. Bernasconi (Contraves AG, Zurich, Switzerland), E.Pagana, G.Reibaldi. GLOBECOM '85. IEEE Global Telecommunications Conference. Conference Record. Communication Technology to Provide New Services (Cat.No.85CH2190-7), New Orleans, LA, USA, 2-5 Dec. 1985 (New York, USA: IEEE 1985), p 407-11 vol.1 — Abstract

54358 Electronic tracking feed using peripheral horns suitable for front fed antennas. E.C.Johnston, G.Alatsatianos (British Telecom Int., London, England), B.Watson, S.McLaren.
IEE Colloquium on 'Recent Advances in Microwave Satellite Sub Systems' (Digest No.78), London, England, 19 May 1986 (London, England, IEE 1986), p.2/1-4. — Abstract

39398 Teleoperation of robot for maintenance and inspection in the containment vessel of nuclear power plant. S.Hosaka, T.Ohmichi (Takasago Tech.Inst., Mitsubishi Heavy Ind.Ltd., Japan).
Proceedings of '85 International Conference on Advanced Robotics, Tokyo, Japan, 9-10 Sept. 1985 (Tokyo, Japan, Japan Ind. Robot Assoc., 1985), p.379-86. — Abstract

39388 Experience in the transfer of nuclear engineering technology.
T.A. Bower (General Electric Co., San Jose, CA, USA).
Trans. Am. Nucl. Soc., (USA), vol.51, p.224-5 (1986). (Transactions of the Third International Conference on Nuclear Technology Transfer: ICONTT-III, Madrid, Spain, 14-15 Oct. 1985) — Abstract

39395 Fusion energy development at McDonnell Douglas: why and how.
W.B.Ard, (McDonnell Douglas Astronaut Co., St.Louis, MO, USA).
Proceedings of the 20th International Energy Conversion Engineering Conference. Energy for the Twenty-First Century, Miami Beach, FL, USA, 18-23 Aug.1985 (Warrendale, PA, USA: SAE 1985), p.36-7 vol.3 —Abstract

37370 Electronic mail: the new way to communicate.
9th International Online Information Meeting, London, England, 3-5 Dec, 1985. (Abingdon, Oxford, England: Learned Inf. 1985), p.323-30. — Abstract

Knowledge Representation for Decision Support Systems. Proceedings of the IFIP WG 8.3 Working Conference, Durham, England, 24-26 July 1984 (Amsterdam, Netherlands: North-Holland 1985), p.161-6 — Abstract

Library and information science abstracts

85/6254
Online information retrieval systems in southern Africa: current situation, problems and development trends. A.M. Dippenaar, D.W. Fokker, H. Bruin. In: *8th International Online Information Meeting, London, 4-6 December 1984* 105-113, table, 2 refs. — Abstract

46

Information vom Standpunkt des wissenschaftlichen Verlages. [Information from the scientific publisher's viewpoint.] Wilhelm Schwabl. In, *Symposium Mittelfristige Perspektiven einer nationalen Informationspolitik. Wien, 5-6 April 1984* [*Symposium Mid-term view of a national information policy, Vienna, 5-6 April 1984*] 4 (special edition) 1984, 39-40. — Abstract

Fig. 4.4 continued

Engineering index

070039 LUMINESCENCE STUDIES OF INTERACTING METAL COMPLEXES IN TWO DIMENSIONS — Abstract

Patterson, Howard H. (Univ. of Maine at Orono, Orono, ME, USA); Roper, Gerald; Biscoe, John; Ludi, Andreas; Blom, Nils. *J Lumin* v 31-32 pt 1 and 2 Dec 1984, Proc of the 1984 Int Conf on Lumin, Madison, WI, USA, Aug 13-17 1984 p 555-557.

070040 INTERSTITIAL ATOMS IN METAL-METAL BONDED ARRAYS: THE SYNTHESIS AND CHARACTERIZATION OF HEPTASCANDIUM DECACHLORODICARBIDE, $Sc_7Cl_{10}C_2$, AND COMPARISON WITH THE INTERSTITIAL-FREE Sc_7Cl_{10} — Abstract

Hwu,Shiou-Jyh (Iowa State Univ, Ames Lab, Ames, IA, USA). Corbett, John D.; Poeppelmeier, Kenneth R. *J Solid State Chem* v 57 n 1 Mar 15 1985, Symp on Met-Met Bonding in Solid State Clusters and Ext Arrays, St.Louis, MO, USA, Apr 9-10 1984 p 43-58.

4.5 Citation of other assorted materials

Various other types of document may from time to time be cited in an abstracting or indexing publication. Formats such as microforms, patents and machine-readable data are perhaps the most likely. These should be handled in a manner consistent with the more predominant forms of document in the publication. Also, sound recordings, samples, maps and graphic materials may occasionally merit inclusion. A suitable framework for the citation of such materials is the ISBD(G).

This chapter has introduced some of the problems and standards associated with bibliographical references, and should prove helpful to the new abstractor or indexer. International standards have been mentioned where relevant standards exist, and their adoption is strongly recommended. However, this work cannot be prescriptive since local citation practices must be accepted by the individual abstractor or indexer. Actual practices may deviate from internationally agreed norms, but it is to be hoped that they will do so in the future only for some sound reason.

Chapter 5

INDEXING

The objective of any index is to be able to retrieve the records or documents that have been stored and organized by the indexing process. The next few chapters concentrate on some important aspects of indexing, but it is important to remember that an index is of any value only if information and documents can be satisfactorily traced. The indexing process creates a description of a document or information, usually in some recognized and accepted style or format. Successful retrieval hangs on the searcher being able to reconstruct that document description when he wants to locate the document again. Indexing, and later searching, centre upon the matching of document profiles. Two points cannot be too strongly emphasized:

(a) the searcher needs to appreciate indexing principles in order to enhance the possibility that he will bring the appropriate document or information profile to the index
(b) the indexer must consider the index's potential audience.

5.1 Subject indexing and analysis
The first half of this work dealt with abstracting. Abstracting is an attempt to present a summary of document content. Indexing also hinges upon this objective, but, because index terms must be used as access points, the summarization of document content achieved in indexing documents must be more tightly structured. An index might, in the interests of establishing a framework for discussion be defined as: 'an organized series of access points which lead from information known to the user to additional previously unknown information'.

An index normally hinges on a series of headings or access or entry points arranged in some recognizable order. Each access point is supplemented by some other information which is designed to indicate where further information or document details may be located. An author index, for instance, comprises a series of alphabetically organized author names. Usually each of these names will be accompanied by document reference numbers or classification numbers and document citations. Here, however, the main concern is subject indexes, and those subject indexes based upon alphabetical subject headings. Such subject indexes are a series of index records with each record incorporating a word or phrase describing the subject acting as the access point, and further details. These details are likely to include the title and/or citation of the appropriate works, and may be supported by more complete details in another list.

Some indexes are printed and published. Others are in-house indexes compiled for the exclusive use of information staff, and yet other indexes are stored on a computer and must be searched by communicating with the computer store via a terminal. Computer-based systems, in particular, permit a wider range of index styles and approaches than some manual indexes or printed indexes. Computer searching has many facilities and permits a more flexible approach to index searching, but printed indexes have the advantage of ease of perusal. Much will be said later about the merits and drawbacks of the various types of index and approaches to indexing, but this chapter highlights the common features of a good index. All effective indexes must have some common facets if only because the audience does not alter merely because the indexer chooses to pursue certain indexing practices. An index, whatever theory it reflects, must be comprehensible to the majority of its users.

All indexes must cater for the variety of potential approaches to a subject. Two categories of problem arise from this fundamental need:

(a)   the indexer must label or name the subject effectively
(b)   the indexer must find some avenue by which to signal the relationships between subjects so that search strategies may evolve.

The first category of problem, the naming of the subject, involves consideration of the following posers.

1   Synonyms are terms with the same or similar meanings. Near synonyms are common; two terms rarely have precisely the same meaning, but two terms may be regarded as equivalent for some purposes. For example, in a general index salaries, wages and income may be regarded as equivalent, but in an index devoted to taxation, it may be important to differentiate between these terms and their associated concepts. Some subjects have both common and technical names, e.g. salt or sodium chloride, or names which represent changes in usage over time, e.g. wireless, radio, transistor. Other subjects may be treated as synonymous in that they all have the same stem, e.g. sterilizer, sterilizing and sterilized. The merging of synonyms carries implications for effectiveness of the index in terms of precision and recall (see last section in this chapter).

2   Homographs are words which have the same spelling as each other, but diverse meanings. Their meaning is usually established by context. Examples of homographs are: bear (to carry, or an animal) and score (music, football or to cut).

3   All nouns have a plural and singular form. Are both to be included

in the index, and if so, what is the distinction between the two forms?

4 Subjects that can be described only with terms comprising more than one word, e.g. merchant ships, pressure vessels, algebraic topology, present a difficulty. Whichever word in the term is used as the main entry point in an index an index user might choose to seek the subject under the other word or words used in the subject description. Inversion may group like subjects, but damages predictability; yet it must be considered.

5 Composite subjects present the same family of problem as multiple-word terms, but there may be many unit concepts, and rather more than two or three words. Here, citation order becomes even more vital. For example, 'an encyclopaedia of bibliography' is not 'a bibliography of encyclopaedias'. The same two terms 'bibliography' and 'encyclopaedias' may describe both; only the order in which they appear will distinguish one topic from the other. Here we are moving into the realms of syntactic relationships.

The second category of problem revolves around the specification of relationships. There are two main categories of relationship, viz. semantic and syntactic relationships. Syntactic relationships arise from the syntax of the document which is undergoing analysis, and derive solely from literary warrant. For example, a document on 'the cutting of glass-fibre-reinforced plastics for use in the hulls of yachts' draws together the concepts: cutting, glass-fibre-reinforced plastics, hulls and yachts. Any of these concepts may also emerge in other contexts where the existence of the relationships defined in this document is irrelevant. Other vessels in addition to yachts may have hulls, and a number of other materials or objects may be subjected to cutting. These relationships must be evident in an index. Semantic relationships are equally important. They show the aspects of genus—species relationships and reflect assumed and well-recognized hierarchies. For example, 'expansion' is always a type of 'dimensional change'. A thorough indexer will make provision for links between two such related topics.

These then are the problems that any index must recognize and attempt to overcome. We move on to consider the process by which indexing is accomplished.

5.2 The indexing process
The documentation concerning indexing is in danger of presenting a biased view of indexing. Information retrieval texts, and this work is no exception, tend to be preoccupied with indexing languages and the techniques of index construction and their evaluation. This approach does insufficient justice to the preliminary steps in the indexing process. Indexing, in fact, involves at least three stages:

Familiarization—▶Analysis—▶Conversion of concepts to index terms

The objective in performing these three stages, which will each be considered more fully in the next few paragraphs, is to construct a document profile. Index records and database keys can be derived from this document profile. Most documents have many characteristics that might function as search keys. A complete set of possible search keys can be described as a document profile. Some keys are straightforward to assign. Those keys signifying the document origins, e.g. authors' names, present relatively few problems, but subject content keys are more difficult. All of the problems mentioned in the previous section must be taken into consideration. In addition, the appropriate set of search keys will be a function of the audience for whom the index is designed.

The first step towards a successful index or set of search keys is familiarization. The indexer must become conversant with the subject content of the document, in just the same way as an abstractor must immerse himself in the text. The difference is only that an indexer is not usually called upon to appreciate the subtleties of the subject to the same extent as an abstractor. In order to achieve good consistent indexing the indexer must, however, have a thorough appreciation of the structure of the subject and the nature of the contribution that the document makes to the advancement of knowledge. Plainly, the familiarization stage is circumvented in a computer-based indexing system with machine-assigned terms.

Analysis is a second stage prior to index-term selection. the human analysis of a document and decisions concerning which subjects are sufficiently significant for indexing are difficult to codify. Some features of the process can be specified, but others rely to a large extent upon experience and intuition. To some extent, at least, any theory designed to study this process evolves from practice rather than vice versa. Some topics in documents represent the main theme of the document. This obviously must be represented in indexing, but to what extent need minor or secondary themes be indexed? Aspects of this dilemma will be considered in the last section in this chapter and it is clear that the concepts that must be recognized at this stage depend upon the anticipated use of the final index. Sometimes guidelines are provided that may go some way towards instructing indexers in consistent identification of concepts. *Chemical abstracts* indexers, for example, are instructed to index: 'every measurement, observation, method, apparatus, suggestion and theory that is presented as new and of value in itself; all new chemical compounds and all elements, compounds and other substances for which new data are given'. This instruction bears out the earlier statement that the identification of concepts is related to the subject undergoing indexing. (Note: 'analysis' here is used in a restricted sense. Analysis can be used to mean all of the processes involved in the construction of a document profile of any kind, and might incorporate cataloguing, indexing, classifying and abstracting.)

Once the preliminary analysis of the concepts present in a document has been completed the indexer may proceed to select terms which match the concepts to be indexed, from an index vocabulary. This topic is the concern of Chapter 6. The three main stages of the indexing process need not necessarily be completed sequentially. An indexer who is familiar with a given indexing language, in particular, may think in the terms of the language, and thus may be capable of accomplishing the three stages concurrently.

5.3 Indexing languages

An indexing language is the language used to describe subject or other aspects of information or documents in an index. In this work emphasis is on alphabetical indexing languages, and classification is altogether neglected. (For an exploration of classification theory see Buchanan, B., *Theory of library classification*, London, Bingley, 1979.) Aspects of indexing languages will be developed in Chapters 6 and 7. Here we will consider merely the main categories of indexing languages. The three main categories are as follows.

1 *Controlled indexing languages* form a category into which fall subject headings lists (including Sears' List of Subject Headings, the Library of Congress List of Subject Headings, Subject Headings in Engineering (SHE), and thesauri, many of which are modelled on the Engineers' Joint Council Thesaurus). Terms that are acceptable for use in indexes based on the controlled language are shown in a list. The indexer selects and assigns terms to documents in accordance with this prescribed list of terms. The terms listed in the accepted category may be form indicators such as language, or type of document, but will mostly be subject descriptors. Controlled languages are usually used in systems with human assignment of indexing terms. It is, however, possibly to specify the list of terms that a computer should assign if they are present in a document. In this type of machine-assigned indexing the language is controlled (i.e. the terms that are to be used), but the occasions on which the terms may be used are not.

2 *Free indexing languages* cannot be as easily delimited as controlled indexing languages. It is the nature of a free indexing language that any word or term that suits the subject may be assigned as an indexing term. The terms may be computer- or human-assigned although free-language indexing is commonest in a computer-indexing environment. The computer operates by indexing under every word with which it is provided unless expressly instructed to do otherwise.

3 *Natural-language indexing* is indexing that uses the language of the document. It is plainly one type of free-language indexing. Most natural-language indexing is concerned with the computer-assignment of terms, and is based upon the language of title, abstract and other text of records.

Selection is simple and there is no need for scanning and analysis of documents. There is still active debate as to whether natural-language indexing leads to effective retrieval.

All three of the above types of indexing languages are possibilities for index construction. Some rely more heavily upon the skills of the indexer at the input stage, whilst others call upon greater searching skills. The diversity of indexing practices and approaches and the very fact that all three types are to be found in operation simultaneously in some indexing applications illustrate that the debate as to which is the most effective has not been positively settled. Indeed it is often proposed that most effective retrieval can be achieved by judicious use of a combination of these indexing language types.

5.4 Indexing systems

Indexing systems are the means whereby an indexing language may be employed to create an index or other search device. An indexing system is, then: 'a set of prescribed procedures for organizing the contents of records of knowledge for the purposes of retrieval and dissemination'.

Indexing systems can be divided into two categories according to the way in which they handle composite subjects. Composite subjects are subjects that comprise a number of distinct single concepts. The first type of indexing system, pre-coordinate indexing, attempts to treat composite subjects as units, and rests on integrated subject descriptions. The terms for each of the single concepts are selected from the indexing language and arranged in an order dictated by the language and the system. The resultant heading represents the subject as a whole and an entry can be filed under the heading for any document which matches the heading. Thus, typical headings might be:

- Mining: Slag heaps: Planting: Grass, Metal tolerant
- Housing: Heating: Equipment: Paint: Spraying, Electrostatic programmers.

During searching the index user is expected to formulate headings in the same way, and hopefully to match his subject description with the indexer's description. Obviously, there is plenty of scope for mismatch. The searcher may very legitimately approach the index from one of the concepts which is not represented as the lead term (such as, above, Planting or Paint). Thus, the indexer in designing a pre-coordinate index is anxious to:

(a) quote the individual concepts in a composite subject in an order which is helpful to the maximum number of users
(b) select a mechanism for generating additional references or access points entries which will provide access from other components of the heading

53

These two problems are explored in Chapter 9. As will become apparent in Chapter 9, pre-coordinate indexing is especially but not solely appropriate for printed indexes.

Post-coordinate indexing is one attempt to avoid the problems associated with the combination of single concepts into a heading for a composite subject. The process of analysis and the selection of terms is little different, but the index records as stored no longer combine these terms. Instead, descriptions of appropriate documents are stored in association with each single concept term. This approach will create relatively lengthy lists of documents linked to each term. Searching, then, must offer some means of coordinating or combining concepts. Thus, coordination of concepts occurs at the search stage; hence, post-coordinate indexing or coordinate indexing. Pre-coordinate indexing, in stark contrast, indicates that coordination must also be conducted with this approach but that coordination is considered prior to the creation of the index rather than after. The same two documents as are noted above might in a post-coordinate index be listed under the following individual terms:

Mining	Housing
Slag heaps	Heating
Painting	Equipment
Grass	Paint
Metal tolerant	Spraying
	Electrostatic programmers

Index entries and headings are plainly simpler than in a pre-coordinate system, but the combination of terms at the searching stage may offer various pitfalls. Post-coordinate indexing is important in computer-based information retrieval systems.

Whichever indexing language or system is favoured, and whether terms are assigned by computer or human the document becomes labelled with a set of words that constitute a document profile. A search question can also be expressed using the same terms and structuring. It is desirable that the search profile and the index profile be framed in the same style. Thus, a system based on controlled-language document profiles must be searched with the search profiles constructed from the same controlled language. We consider searching further in the next section when some simple parameters for the evaluation of indexing languages and systems are reviewed.

5.5 Measures of index effectiveness
This section considers a few devices with which it is possible to gauge the effectiveness of an index or set of search keys. Only those concepts that are vital to a clear appreciation of the indexing process are introduced.

For any user who approaches an index or computerized information-retrieval system there are a number of records in the system that are relevant to the topic of his search and the remainder which are of no interest. Even for those items that are relevant some may be judged to be highly relevant whilst others may be partially relevant and yet others may be only marginally relevant. For example, an index user may desire information on diesel engines, and there may be records for documents in the index that deal specifically with this topic which will be selected as being highly relevant. However, although subject is a primary consideration in the assessment of relevance, this is not the only factor that determines whether a user wishes to be alerted to the existence of a document. A user may reject a document because it is in a language that he cannot read or because it was written too long ago.

Consider again those documents indexed by the system that may be partially relevant to a search. Suppose our reader is interested in diesel engines, but there is only a limited quantity of material directly concerned with this topic. However, it is possible to broaden the search and find additional information on diesel engines by retrieving documents on engines and extracting from these documents any sections on diesel engines. The result will be the recall of more information, but in order to trace this information it has been necessary to retrieve more documents from the index, and in the process retrieve documents that are not relevant. These non-relevant documents are frequently described as 'noise'. Notice that it is possible to improve recall indefinitely by scanning the entire document collection, but that this will be achieved only by a drop in the proportion of relevant documents. There are then two conflicting objectives to any search. Ideally, we would like to maximize recall, or the number of relevant documents retrieved, at the same time as ensuring that the documents that are retrieved all remain relevant. Partly because of the fact that documents have shades of relevance to a given topic this is an impossible objective.

The concepts introduced in the above few paragraphs have been more precisely defined in an experimental situation. The following definitions embody some of the ideas above:

$$\text{Recall ratio} = \frac{\text{Number of relevant documents retrieved}}{\text{Number of relevant documents in the system}} \times 100\%$$

$$\text{Precision ratio} = \frac{\text{Number of relevant documents retrieved}}{\text{Total number of documents retrieved}} \times 100\%$$

The more specific way of stating the relationship between these two parameters is to say that they are inversely related, i.e. as one improves the other must decrease. The practical application of these measures is

55

hindered by the difficulty encountered in evaluating some of the features. For example, without scanning the entire system it is impossible to estimate the total number of relevant documents in the system.

Since it is not possible, in general, to achieve full recall at the same time as full precision, the indexer must design an index to give the correct balance of the two. The desirable balance will depend upon the audience. Normally a user will be satisfied with a few items on the topic, as long as they are relevant and meet his other criteria such as language and level. Here high precision, but low recall is satisfactory. Sometimes, though, a user wants every document or piece of information on a topic traced, and then high recall must be sought at the cost of low precision and much noise. The best indexing system can respond to these various demands.

Recall and precision interact with other features of the system. Specificity is one aspect of a system that must be settled. Specificity is the extent to which the system permits the indexer to be precise about the subject of a document. A completely specific statement of document content would constitute the document itself, but obviously a more formalized approach is sought in an index. In any index a level of specificity is settled and the indexer then assigns terms that are as specific as the system allows. It is as well to note the connection between specificity and recall and precision. The higher the specificity of indexing the more likely it is that search outputs will show high precision. Lower specificity will be associated with lower precision but higher recall. In our search for diesel engines if the term diesel engine does not exist in the system then we must search under the broader term engines. Documents can be identified as relevant only by scanning the rather larger number of documents listed under the broader heading.

Exhaustivity of indexing also has some impact on recall and precision. Most documents have more than one theme. The indexer is faced with the choice of which of the themes of the document to provide access to via an index. Exhaustivity concerns the number of themes that are indexed in a document, or can usually be measured by the number of index terms assigned to a document. The stock of a general library is often represented by only one or two entries in a catalogue for each document. A more specialized collection may be identified and indexed in one document. The indexer must judge which themes are worth indexing. In contrast to specificity, exhaustivity increases precision at the cost of recall. If the subthemes in documents are indexed these documents will be retrieved, yet will discuss the topic being sought only in a secondary position. Thus, less relevant documents will also be retrieved, and are more likely to be retrieved than in an index that provides access only to main topics in documents. Equally, recall is improved by high exhaustivity since all documents that mention a topic regardless of the extent of the discussion of the topic will be retrieved.

Chapter 6

CONTROLLED INDEXING LANGUAGES

6.1 The nature of controlled indexing languages

Chapter 5 introduced the concept of an index language and placed the concept in context. This chapter develops the theme of indexing languages by studying a specific type of indexing language, a controlled indexing language. The chapter will concentrate upon the way in which a controlled indexing language is embodied in a thesaurus.

Control is necessary in respect of the tems used in an index because of the variety of natural language. Such control may involve the barring of certain terms from use as index headings or access points. Terms which are to be used are likely to be specified, and synonyms recognized and possibly eliminated (for example, perhaps 'packaging' is to be used rather than 'wrapping'). Preferred word forms will also be noted: 'heat' may be preferred to 'hot'. The easiest way to exercise this type of control over index terms is to list or store the acceptable terms in a vocabulary. Such lists will embody both specific decisions concerning the preferred words, and also, by example, decisions relating to the form of words to be used, e.g. singular or plural, noun or adjective. A thesaurus is such a list. A more formal definition of a thesaurus might be: 'an organized list of terms from a specialized vocabulary, which has been arranged to facilitate the selection of index terms'.

Terms from an indexing language may be assigned in one of three ways:

    1   analytically, or by a human indexer who analyses subject content and selects and assigns index terms which accurately reflect subject content;

    2   clerically, or by a human indexer selecting terms clerically according to some prescribed procedure. For example all significant words in the title and first two lines of the abstract of a document may form the basis for the indexing of that document. The human indexer works mechanically and rapidly; he should require no insight into the document content;

    3   automatically, or by a computer selecting terms from titles, abstracts or the full text of the document.

Thesauri of various types may feature in indexing systems based on any of these approaches to the assignment of index terms. For the sake of simplicity this chapter will concentrate on the type of thesaurus normally associated with the analytical assignment of index terms, and extracts from various such thesauri are shown in Appendix 6.1. Nevertheless, many of the themes introduced in the next few sections can be applied in other indexing environments. Although not identical, thesauri appropriate for computer-indexing systems have much in common with systems where index terms are humanly assigned. The student, after an initial reading of this chapter, should re-examine many of the ideas that are presented in the next several pages and consider their applicability to computer-indexing and searching.

A thesaurus summarizes an indexing language. It is too easy to assume that as such a thesaurus is of interest only to indexers. This is not the case. Selection of index terms, the key function of a thesaurus, is an essential element of both searching and indexing. The thesaurus aims to achieve some or better coincidence between the vocabulary of an indexer and the vocabulary used by a searcher. In the same way that an indexer must consider alternative index terms in indexing, the searcher will miss relevant documents if alternative index terms are not sought during retrieval. A simple example will serve to emphasize this point.

Example
An enquirer wishes to retrieve documents on the 'finishing of concrete floors for industrial buildings'. Obvious access points in an index would be:

Finishing
Concrete
Floors
Industrial buildings

But some of these terms may not be used in the index because they are not preferred terms in the index language used in the index. Other terms may yield few relevant references, and it may be necessary to seek references under related headings. A thesaurus might advise the searcher that the following alternative terms might prove fruitful:

Coating
Polishing
Cement
Factories
other more specific terms, e.g. Printing works.

A more extensive search under these additional terms may well prove more thorough and profitable.

Most thesauri comprise one or more lists and displays of terms. The next section considers the basic alphabetical list of terms at the heart of a thesaurus. Subsequent sections look at other aspects of thesauri and thesaurus construction. Most thesauri are designed to fit a specific set of objectives. They are tailored to meet the specification inherent in a given application, hence the emphasis on thesaurus construction in the penultimate section. Thesauri have been used to index specialized collections of documents, abstracts, bulletins, current-awareness tools, SDI systems and a variety of other bibliographical tools. In many applications the information officer can expect to be responsible for compiling an in-house thesaurus. Nevertheless, an examination of some of the common features of existing published thesauri is an appropriate preliminary study.

6.2 The main thesaurus listing of terms

The main list of index terms is the core of the thesaurus and can be expected to feature in any thesaurus however elementary or unrefined. This listing usually contains, in one alphabetically ordered sequence:

- descriptors, or terms which are acceptable for use in indexes to describe concepts
- non-descriptors, or terms that are *not* to be used in the index, but which appear in the thesaurus in order to expand the entry vocabulary (the entry words) of the indexing language
- some display of relationships between terms, and by implication, concepts.

Index terms
This section deals with the nature of the terms that are accepted for inclusion in a thesaurus. Most index terms in a thesaurus are 'uniterms', or single-concept terms. The form of these terms, whether descriptors or non-descriptors, is usually one of the following:

- single words, e.g. Government, Hovercraft, Housing
- phrases of two or three words, often comprising a noun and an adjective, e.g. Western languages, Hydraulic excavators, Power stations
- two words linked by 'and' or '&', e.g. Fixtures and fittings
- compound phrases, e.g. Linear-time dependent dead-time control systems
- names of persons, bodies, places, e.g. Laboratory of the Government Chemist, MEDLARS, Manchester.

Concepts should be described as simply as possible whilst retaining compatibility with normal usage. Thus, single-word terms or, failing these, two-word terms, are preferred for describing concepts if such terms exist. Single words are likely to encourage a high level of coincidence between the terminology of the indexer and that of the searcher.

The index terms may stand alone but are sometimes defined more precisely by the use of both qualifiers and scope notes. Qualifiers function as an integral part of the index term, so that index terms of the form:

Storage (Stock)
Planning (Libraries)

are created. Scope notes are brief explanations shown in juxtaposition to some index terms in the thesaurus. These scope notes define the intended use of the index term. Scope notes are sometimes differentiated by the abbreviation SN (standing for scope note). Two examples are:

(a) Full text: (the text of documents; natural language, e.g. as a source of information/data retrieval)

(b) Absorber: SN−Process equipment (When cited only to indicate that the equipment is used, index process instead.)

Relationships

Relationships between the terms in an indexing language are also indicated in most published thesauri. These relationships can be viewed as belonging to one of three main categories: preferential, affinitive or hierarchical. Each category of relationship is considered in turn.

Preferential relationships generally indicate preferred terms or descriptors and thus perform the vital function of controlling index vocabulary, by specifying which terms are to be used in the index and which are not. Statements conveying preferential relationships imply that some terms are to be treated as synonymous. The indexer must evaluate whether any given concepts can satisfactorily be treated as equivalent, or whether the index user will profit if a distinction is made between two kindred terms. The effect upon search recall and precision, as well as other measures of retrieval effectiveness, must be taken into account in deciding whether or not to merge any two synonyms or potential synonyms.

Preferential relationships are indicated by statements of the form:

A is not authorized; *see* B instead

where A and B are two index terms, A a non-descriptor, and B a descriptor. This type of statement in its simplest form will cater for:

- synonyms, e.g. Disabilities *use* Handicaps
- antonyms, e.g. Temperance *see* Intemperance
  Temperance *use* Intemperance
- spelling variants, e.g. Labor *see* Labour
- abbreviations, e.g. Polyvinyl Chloride *use* PVC
- specific to general (i.e. specific term not authorized, use a more general term), e.g. Alsatians *use* Dogs.

There are two variations on the basic statement of a preferential relationship. The first of these is:

A not authorized; *see* B and C instead.

This provision is a means of indicating index-term selection for complex subjects. The statement below, for example, suggests that in indexing or searching for information on 'staff salaries' the two terms 'costing' and 'staff' should be searched in coordination with each other:

TC Costing *and* Staff (Staff salaries)

The Thesaurus of the American Petroleum Institute caters for a similar situation by instructions of the type:

Absorption Tube
 Use Tube
  Plus absorber

The second variation on the basic statement of a preferential relationship is:

A not authorized; *see* B or C or. . . N instead.

This kind of statement is appropriate when a general term (here A) is not included as a preferred term in the list, and works on narrower but related subjects are to be indexed under a suitable more specific term (here B, C. . . N). An example of such a statement is:

Programming languages *see* FORTRAN, ALGOL, COBOL

The statement above may also be used to divert the user from a homograph to more explicit terms. For instance:

Lead *see* Electrical connectors; Metallic lead.

All statements indicating preferential relationships will usually appear in both direct and inverted forms. Thus, the thesaurus user may approach a term 'from either direction'. Thus a statement such as:

Alsatians *use* Dogs

should be complemented by the inverse statement:

Dogs *UF* Alsatians.

(UF is a common abbreviation for 'Use For').
The Medical Subject Headings (MeSH) entry:

MOUTH FLOOR
 x Floor of mouth
 x Sublingual region

should be supported by entries under 'Floor of mouth' and 'Sublingual region'.

Hierarchical relationships may be represented in the thesaurus by statements which take the form:

A is permitted, but consider using B or C or...N instead

where, as before, A,B,C...N are index terms, and B and C are related to A via some hierarchy of relationships. Hierarchical relationships must be indicated in order that users may make the transition from a first access point to related terms or access points. The indication of these relationships helps the indexer to select the most specific term to describe a concept that is available in the thesaurus. The searcher is kept informed as to related terms under which additional information or documents may have been indexed. Hierarchical relationships take one of two forms, depending upon whether A is subordinate to B, C...N, or B, C...N are subordinate to A. Broader terms are generally indicated by the abbreviation 'BT'. For example:

Analysis
    BT Mathematics

suggests that Analysis is a subordinate topic to Mathematics, or that Analysis is a branch of Mathematics.

Narrower terms are signified by the abbreviation 'NT'. In the following statement:

Analysis
    NT Differential calculus

notes that Differential calculus is an aspect of Analysis.

In most cases it is appropriate that 'BT' and 'NT' statements go in pairs. Thus the above statement should be complemented by:

Differential calculus
    BT Analysis

Affinitive relationships are a further type of connection between index terms, and thus may be codified by a similar statement to the statement that has been considered above in respect of hierarchical relationships. Again, the following statement is appropriate:

A is permitted, but consider B or C or ...N, as well or instead.

The distinction between affinitive and hierarchical relationships lies in the rather less structured nature of affinitive relationships. Affinitive relationships exist between terms that are not necessarily connected to one another in any fixed hierarchical manner. Affinitive relationships are often indicated by the code 'RT', standing for 'Related Term'. For example, Instruction is a related concept to Education, Teaching, and Courses:

Instruction
  RT Education
    Teaching
    Courses

An alternative means of expressing an affinitive relationship is found in MeSH. The term 'see related' is the equivalent of 'RT'. Thus, the following is an extract from MeSH:

Personality development
  see related
    Child development
    Growth
    Socialization

All means of conveying affinitive relationships list a number of terms which may be used, both by the indexer and the searcher, as well as, or instead of, the original entry term.

It is usual for 'RT' to be reflexive and the above example concerning Instruction would be accompanied by a series of inverted statements of the form:

Education
  RT Instruction

On those occasions when it is not deemed desirable to provide access in both directions 'SA', to signify 'See also' may be used as a non-reflexive version of 'RT'. The following might be appropriate:

Courses
  SA Education

Some of the more common means of indicating relationships in thesauri have been reviewed in the last few paragraphs. It is important to remember that such relationships are recorded in the thesaurus, and are not always transferred from the thesaurus to any index. For effective use of the index the searcher, as well as the indexer, should refer to the thesaurus. In applications where a thesaurus is not likely to be available to the index searcher it is necessary to transfer relationships recognized in a thesaurus to the indexes that are based on the thesaurus.

6.3 Display of relationships

Some display of relationships appears in the main alphabetical list to the thesaurus. Many thesauri attempt a further display of relationships. Such displays may summarize relationships which are not evident from the main alphabetical list, or reiterate the relationships already stated in the main alphabetical list in a different format. Any type of more extensive relationship display is more likely to be incorporated into a printed and/or published thesaurus than in locally generated thesauri, which are restricted to one or two applications. Indexers responsible for in-house thesauri are less likely to have the time to produce displays. Further, these indexers are probably so familiar with their subject area that they, whether in the guise of indexer or searcher, will profit little from any additional guides to relationships. Some of the devices that can and have been used in the display of relationships are shown below.

Hierarchical displays may form a separate section of the thesaurus. The hierarchical relationships associated with selected index terms may be revealed by displaying related terms beneath such terms in a supplementary list in the thesaurus. The degree to which a term is inset in the list indicates its position in the hierarchy. Those terms which are used as the starting point, or most general term, in a hierarchical display are sometimes designated 'highest terms', and coded 'HT'. In the Thesaurus of Scientific and Engineering Terms, any term in the main alphabetical listing which has no 'BT' references, and at least two levels of 'NT' references is tabulated in the hierarchical index. The display in the hierarchical index shows all terms related to the main term, either directly, or at one or more removes from it, by an 'NT' reference.

Categorized displays are useful in thesauri covering subject fields that constitute a number of distinct subfields. Thesaurus terms are entered under a series of category headings. All terms may be organized in this way, or, alternatively, only a representative sample of the terms may be categorized. MeSH, for example, has a categorized list in which over one half of the terms in the alphabetical list are entered in the ordered list. These categorized lists could be described as very crude classifications of the topics covered by the thesaurus. Categorized displays are intended to provide the thesaurus user with an overview of the structure of the relationships between terms.

Permuted listings of terms, sometimes referred to as KWIC listings, are valuable in permitting access to the second, third, fourth or any subsequent word in a multi-word term. By accident of alphabetical arrangement these permuted listings may also group different branches of the same subject that might be scattered when entered under their first word. In a permuted listing every word in a multi-word term is brought, in turn, into the access position (as in a KWIC index; see Chapter 7). So, for example, the following two word terms will be listed both under their first words, and under their second words. The part of the sequence which shows the second words will give a grouping around the word 'Chemistry', of the type:

Biological Chemistry
Inorganic Chemistry

Organic   Chemistry
Physical   Chemistry.

The ERIC Thesaurus has a permuted listing, known as the rotated descriptor display. Educational terminology is rife with concepts that are best described with pre-coordinated terms. Since few inverted headings are permitted in a thesaurus there is a need to reveal the hidden words in these pre-coordinated terms if poor search performance is to be avoided.

Graphic displays are an intriguing step towards a multi-dimensional pictorial map of the subject areas covered by a thesaurus. Usually several linked displays, each occupying one page, will be drafted for each thesaurus, each display covering a subfield within the topic of the thesaurus. A number of graphic display devices have been proposed, and there is scope for further imagination. Given below are some of the display devices that have been incorporated into published thesauri.

1 *Euler circles*   Each concept is defined by a polygonal domain or 'circle'. Synonymous terms, by definition, occupy the same domain and related subjects have overlapping domains. A subject which is perceived as being entirely contained within the bounds of another will have its 'circle' totally within the boundaries of the domain for the broader subject.

2 *Circular thesaurus*   A central concept is shown as a central circle. Related topics are arranged in concentric circles around the central circle. Concepts which are only remotely related to the central concept will be positioned well away from the central circle.

3 *Arrowgraphs* are used in the International Road Research Documentation Scheme (IRRD) Thesaurus to represent the overlap between or the proximity of related subjecs (see figure 6.1). Related terms are joined by arrows leading from general terms out to their more specific partners. The length of the arrow indicates the strength of the association; a shorter arrow between two concepts suggests that the concepts are closely allied.

A full classification scheme, complementary to the thesaurus, is the most thorough means of indicating the relationships between the terms in a thesaurus. All terms may be included, and placed in the most apposite position in the hierarchy of the subject. Many of the more recent thesauri favour this format. Early examples were Thesaurofacet and the London Education Classification. Both boast two sections, a thesaurus and a faceted classification, with the location of any term in both listings being linked by a class number or notation. The notation functions in the same way as it normally does in linking the subject index of a classification scheme to the main classified listing of the scheme. The parallel development of a classification scheme and a thesaurus has much to recommend it; the thesaurus can act as an index to the classified ordering and the hierarchical display of the classification serves as a relationship display for the thesaurus. If both a classification scheme and a thesaurus are required in a given application much effort can be saved by developing a tool which links the two systems. However, this joint venture may not be justifiable unless both a thesaurus and a classification scheme are in demand by one organization at similar times.

In a linked classification scheme and thesaurus, both the thesaurus and the classification scheme have several functions. The thesaurus:

- acts as an index to the classification scheme
- controls synonyms and word forms
- specifies additional related terms, which do not occur in the hierarchy
- permits access to the scheme via a specific term.

The classification scheme, on the other hand:

- permits a broad subject approach
- gives an overview of subjects and relationships
- introduces notation for the scheme.

6.4 Multi-lingual thesauri
Multi-lingual thesauri have always been important for databases or abstracting journal publications where compilation is achieved by a number of distinct agencies engaging on a cooperative venture. Often, one agency may be responsible for covering the literature produced by its country, which may be largely in, say, French, and other agencies will be responsible for literature published in their localities. This literature may be in one of a variety of languages. In order to aid these agencies in indexing the literature that they cover, and so that the database is suitable for use by people with a variety of native tongues, a multi-lingual thesaurus may be compiled. A multi-lingual thesaurus can take several different forms, but typically it is likely to have parallel main alphabetical listings of terms or editions, which cover the different languages represented in the thesauri. Figure 6.1 shows an extract from the International Labour Office Thesaurus, which has listings in English, French and Spanish.

Clearly, a multi-lingual thesaurus has to control the vagaries of not just one natural language, but several. Difficulties arise when equivalent terms do not arise in all languages in which the thesaurus is produced. Sometimes a switching language is introduced. This switching language is a notation that can be used by people or computers to translate terms in all natural languages into, and as an intermediate language between, the various languages. Significant cooperation and communication between the agencies involved with the creation and maintenance of a multi-lingual thesaurus is necessary.

Fig. 6.1 An extract from a multi-lingual thesaurus: The International Labour Office Thesaurus

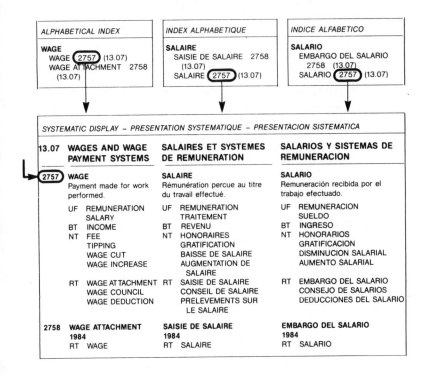

Reproduced with the permission of the International Labour Office. Source: *ILO Thesaurus. Labour, employment and training terminology*, 1985. Copyright © International Labour Organisation, 1985.

6.5 The ROOT thesaurus

Until 1982, when the British Standards Institution published its ROOT thesaurus, although many thesauri adhered to the basic model of a thesaurus as exemplified in the Engineers Joint Council (EJC) Thesaurus, there was no standard, general-purpose thesaurus. The BSI ROOT Thesaurus was developed both as a standard thesaurus which it is hoped will find more and more applications, and also as a thesaurus that could be used by standards organizations, including BSI, to index their own standards. Other users are likely to model their thesauri on the ROOT thesaurus and to extract terms from it for more applications-oriented lists.

The somewhat late arrival of the ROOT thesaurus in the indexing world means that its penetration will be slow, although it has great potential as a tool for standardizing indexing languages.

The second edition was published in 1985, and contains over 12,000 descriptors and 5,500 non-descriptors. The thesaurus is used for the subject indexing of BSI publications on BSI's database, STANDARD-LINE. ROOT descriptors also form the basis of a new printed subject index to the BSI Standards Catalogue. The ROOT thesaurus has been translated into French, German, Czech, Japanese and Portuguese, and is available in both hard-copy and machine-readable forms. The National Youth Bureau's Thesaurus on Youth and the ECOT Thesaurus on Educational Courses and Occupations are examples of thesauri which are being developed in a similar style to the ROOT Thesaurus. The ADLIB software package can produce a thesaurus display in the form of the ROOT Thesaurus.

The ROOT Thesaurus focuses on industrial topics, including measurement, environmental and safety engineering, energy technology and communication. The Thesaurus is available in a printed version, or on magnetic tape. Figure 6.2 shows that there are two lists, a classified list and an alphabetical list, and demonstrates the relationships between these two lists. Note that the alphabetical list shows synonyms, broader terms, narrower terms, and related terms, but these are signalled by different notation from that which has become traditional in thesauri (e.g. UF, BT, NT, RT). The ROOT Thesaurus designations are independent of specific language (i.e. French, German, Italian) and are, therefore, appropriate in a multi-lingual context. The basic designations are:

= which is equivalent to UF
− which is equivalent to USE
< which is equivalent to BT
> which is equivalent to NT
− which is equivalent to RT

6.6 Thesauri and subject headings lists
This work does not discuss traditional subject headings lists such as Sears' List of Subject Headings and Library of Congress List of Subject Headings explicitly. Accounts of such lists are given in the works themselves or such standard texts as Hunter, E. J. and Bakewell, K. G. B., *Cataloguing*, 2nd edition, Bingley, 1983, and Chan, L. M., *Cataloguing and classification: an introduction*, McGraw-Hill, 1981. However, thesauri and subject headings lists share some features. Both thesauri and subject headings lists are preoccupied with:

● controlling the use and form of index terms
● summarizing the relationships between terms in an indexing language.

But, thesauri and subject headings lists achieve these two objectives in different environments. Most of the main subject headings lists are geared to the alphabetical subject approach found in dictionary catalogues. The unique features that distinguish a thesaurus from a subject headings list are primarily:

(a) thesauri are likely to contain terms that are more specific than those found in subject headings lists
(b) thesauri tend to avoid inverted terms (such as Art, French)
(c) headings in thesauri are not subdivided (for instance, Education— bibliographies, would not normally be featured in a thesaurus but headings of this type are common in traditional subject headings lists). Situations where subdivisions may have some utility are catered for by the coordination of index terms.
(d) the relationship display in a thesaurus is often more extensive than the relationship display in a subject headings list
(e) different types of relationships are noted in a thesaurus by the use of RT, NT, and BT, instead of the *see also* which is frequently used to indicate all relationships, whatever their nature, in a subject headings list
(f) the relationships between the terms listed in a thesaurus will often not be transferred to the index. Dictionary catalogues usually contain *see* and *see also* instructions linking related headings
(g) thesauri often boast an additional explicit statement of the structure of the relationships between terms in the form of categorized lists or graphic displays.

6.7 Thesaurus construction

On occasions a published thesaurus will meet the requirements of an information retrieval situation adequately, but in most instances published thesauri are best viewed as models for the library or information unit's own thesaurus. A good thesaurus for any particular application is not necessarily a listing of terms which is well presented, with every relationship identified and a plethora of relationship display devices. The best thesaurus is a tool that has been designed to match the indexing and retrieval environment in which it is called upon to operate. It is therefore important that a librarian or information officer has a thorough understanding of existing thesauri so that they might be not only used in their standard form, but modified to suit local circumstances. Further, an information worker should be capable of constructing a simple thesaurus when the need arises. BS 5723:1979(1984) *Guidelines for the establishment and development of monolingual thesauri* gives advice on the content, layout, methods of construction and maintenance of a monolingual thesaurus.

Fig. 6.2 The ROOT thesaurus—an extract

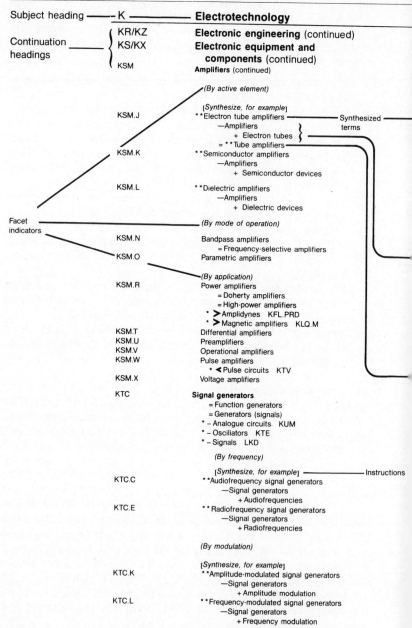

Subject heading —— - K ——————— **Electrotechnology**

Continuation headings
- KR/KZ — **Electronic engineering** (continued)
- KS/KX — **Electronic equipment and components** (continued)
- KSM — **Amplifiers** (continued)

(By active element)

[*Synthesize, for example*]
- KSM.J — **Electron tube amplifiers ——————— Synthesized terms
  - —Amplifiers
  - + Electron tubes
  - = **Tube amplifiers
- KSM.K — **Semiconductor amplifiers
  - —Amplifiers
  - + Semiconductor devices
- KSM.L — **Dielectric amplifiers
  - —Amplifiers
  - + Dielectric devices

Facet indicators

(By mode of operation)
- KSM.N — Bandpass amplifiers
  - = Frequency-selective amplifiers
- KSM.O — Parametric amplifiers

(By application)
- KSM.R — Power amplifiers
  - = Doherty amplifiers
  - = High-power amplifiers
  - * > Amplidynes   KFL.PRD
  - * > Magnetic amplifiers   KLQ.M
- KSM.T — Differential amplifiers
- KSM.U — Preamplifiers
- KSM.V — Operational amplifiers
- KSM.W — Pulse amplifiers
  - * < Pulse circuits   KTV
- KSM.X — Voltage amplifiers

- KTC — **Signal generators**
  - = Function generators
  - = Generators (signals)
  - * – Analogue circuits.   KUM
  - * – Osciliators   KTE
  - * – Signals   LKD

(By frequency)

[*Synthesize, for example*] ——————— Instructions
- KTC.C — **Audiofrequency signal generators
  - —Signal generators
  - + Audiofrequencies
- KTC.E — **Radiofrequency signal generators
  - —Signal generators
  - + Radiofrequencies

(By modulation)

[*Synthesize, for example*]
- KTC.K — **Amplitude-modulated signal generators
  - —Signal generators
  - + Amplitude modulation
- KTC.L — **Frequency-modulated signal generators
  - —Signal generators
  - + Frequency modulation

Reproduced with the permission of the British Standards Institution

70

Electron spectra CRK.FK
  = Electronic spectra
  – Electron emission
  < Spectra COB.Y

**Electron tube amplifiers KSM.J
  — Amplifiers
    + Electron tubes

Electron tube bases
  – Electron tube structure
    KWW.H

Electron tube caps
  – Electron tube structure
    KWW.H

Reciprocal entries

Synonym to synthesized
term

**Tube amplifiers
  — Amplifiers
    —Electron tubes
  =**Electron tube amplifiers KSM.J

Tube heat exchangers NEB.E
  < Heat exchangers

Tubed tyres NTV.TNJ
  < Pneumatic tyres

Amplifiers KSM
  < Electronic equipment and components
  > Audio amplifiers
  > Bandpass amplifiers
  > Differential amplifiers
  > Direct-current amplifiers
  > Operational amplifiers
  > Parametric amplifiers
  > Power amplifiers
  > Preamplifiers
  > Pulse amplifiers
  > Radiofrequency amplifiers
  > Videofrequency amplifiers
  > Voltage amplifiers
  > Wideband amplifiers
  * < Acoustic equipment NME
  * > Rotating amplifiers KFL.PE
  * — Receivers LLP.R
  * — Transponders LLP.PG

Amplifiers
  + Dielectric devices
  =** Dielectric amplifiers KSM.L

Amplifiers
  + Electron tubes
  =** Electron tube amplifiers KSM.J

Amplifiers
  + Semiconductor devices
  =** Semiconductor amplifiers KSM.K

Electron tubes
  + Amplifiers
  =** Electron tube amplifiers KSM.J

Electron tubes
  + Oscillators
  =**Electron tube osciliators KTE.E

Electron-wave tubes KWF
  < Electron tubes
  > Microwave tubes
  * < Thermionic valves KWC
  * < Vacuum tubes KWN

Thesauri have been compiled in a variety of different ways. The following three-step plan identifies the main stages in thesaurus construction. The first two steps, it will be observed, do not involve action, but concentrate upon decision-making. Preliminary decisions such as the anticipated use of the thesaurus and the desirable features of the retrieval language must be taken before plunging into the accumulation of index terms, and analysis of relationships. Appropriate software may be employed to aid in the recording of the thesaurus and even in the collection of terms, but the intellectual effort of planning, term selection and relationship indication remains in the hands of the index system designer.

Step 1: decide the purpose of the thesaurus
Some decisions should be made concerning the anticipated use of the thesaurus. This step involves settling the following parameters as far as possible. There are often problems in identifying all aspects of the use of a thesaurus. This step presents sufficient problems in relation to current use, but when future use is also taken into consideration firm decisions will prove yet more elusive. Nevertheless, as much progress as possible must be made in settling the following;

1 *Subject field* This must be decided by making statements concerning the limits of topic coverage, and the depth to which various aspects of the subject are to be treated. Subject-field definition arises from the scope of the information service or system that the thesaurus is planned to serve. This, in turn, depends upon users and user interests, and it may be necessary to conduct a survey to discover user interests adequately.

2 *Type of literature* This may determine, amongst other features, the amount of detail required. Books, for example, can often demand less specific indexing than periodical articles.

3 *Quantity of literature* The sophistication of a thesaurus and the specificity of its index terms are usually related to the number of documents to be covered by the indexing system for which the thesaurus is intended. In simple terms, the essence of subject organization is the successful division of the literature into manageable categories, each category being associated with one or more index terms. The more documents that an indexing system is expected to embrace, the greater the number of index terms that are likely to be necessary for convenient retrieval. The exact number of document citations that are acceptable under each index term is not absolute and depends on other features of the information system. Some foresight must be employed in order to make realistic speculations as to the eventual size of the collection that will be covered by any index based upon the thesaurus.

4 *Type of information-storage system* This may have implications for the nature of the terms used in the thesaurus. The system may be essentially pre- or post-coordinate, or neither, and terms must be

structured accordingly. An information-storage system which is to be searched by online access to a computer database may require a different range and style of index terms from a system designed primarily to create a printed index.

5 *Resources of the information system* These will impose constraints upon the nature of the thesaurus. There are two types of resources: those necessary and available for initial thesaurus design, and those resources for the development and application of the thesaurus in an indexing environment. Probably the most satisfactory situation is to have adequate resources for initial thesaurus construction to permit the compilation of a high-quality thesaurus. A sound thesaurus will save staff time in operating the indexing system. If staff time and expertise for initial evolution of the thesaurus are scarce, the system can usually function with a less thoroughly refined thesaurus, but extra effort will be necessary when searching the information-retrieval system.

6 *Users* Those who use the information system may influence the explicitness of the detail in a thesaurus. The nature of the users, their type, the frequency with which they use the system and whether users will operate the information system themselves or will use an information officer as an intermediary are all factors to be considered.

7 *Use* The use to which the information system will be put impinges upon most of the earlier issues, but should also be considered in its own right. The number and type of questions posed to the system have implications for the effort that it is worthwhile to divert into thesaurus construction. With few questions and infrequent use it would be more sensible and effective to direct effort into searching, rather than strive for perfection in indexing. Another factor connected with the use of the system is whether the system will be used fundamentally for current-awareness applications, or retrospective retrieval. A thesaurus intended as the tool for current-awareness profile construction may require different terms from a thesaurus which will be used to construct an index covering material issued or published over a number of years.

The implications of all of the above features of the information system must be thoroughly examined before decisions are made concerning the nature of the retrieval language and the thesaurus. For the benefit of all users of the thesaurus who have not had a hand in its initial compilation some written record describing the anticipated use of the thesaurus is valuable.

Step 2: decide the characteristics of the retrieval language and the thesaurus
The purpose of the thesaurus will colour the decisions concerning many of the characteristics of the planned thesaurus. A number of factors need to be considered at this stage, which include the following:

1 *The nature of the language* The relative merits of free, natural and controlled languages need to be evaluated. In particular, it should be noted that an uncontrolled or only partially controlled indexing language shifts the burden of indexing skills to the searcher.

2 *Specificity of the language* This must be appropriate for the application. If the language consists primarily of relatively general terms, the indexer will find difficulty in indexing precisely, and consequently the searcher may have to sift through long lists of document citations. On the other hand very specific index terms may result in items under similar headings being divided and some documents not being retrieved.

3 *Exhaustivity* The number of terms assigned to each document in the indexing system influences the potential specificity of indexing and the retrieval possibilities.

4 *Level of pre-coordination* Many thesauri opt for relatively low levels of pre-coordination, and rely almost entirely upon 'uniterms' or one-concept terms. More complex terms, including those which cover multiple concepts, are permitted only where such terms represent very common concepts within the subject field of the thesaurus. These multiple-concept terms yield greater precision, but are associated with a rather larger indexing language and a higher likelihood of harmful scatter.

Throughout the planning phase the basic language evaluation devices must be taken into account (see Chapter 5).

5 *Thesaurus structure* Once the characteristics of the retrieval language have been agreed, the way in which the language will be encoded in a thesaurus must be decided. A straight alphabetical list must form the core of the thesaurus. Some type of graphic or other relationship display may also be helpful.

Step 3: start to compile the thesaurus
With all planning and preliminary stages completed, the compilation of the thesaurus can begin. This step involves six sub-stages.

1 *Identify the main subject areas* This must be more explicit than may have been required to date. A description of the main subject areas with a careful statement of the content of each forms the skeleton of the main list of terms. Such deliberations on subject will normally generate a preliminary list of significant terms, with those terms collected into groups that reflect the relationships between terms.

2 *Select terms* Once terms have been accepted for inclusion in the thesaurus they must obviously be recorded, so that this sub-stage and the next one must proceed side-by-side. The preliminary list which was compiled in the previous sub-stage must be developed. Synonyms, related terms and other variants must now be collected, either with the aid of machine extraction or intellectually. Humanly-selected terms may be derived from a number of sources. Primary sources of terms are other

lists and documentation in the subject area of the proposed thesaurus, or more specifically:

(a) other thesauri, classification schemes and information-retrieval tools
(b) documents in the subject area, such as periodical articles, indexing and abstracting journals, databases, encyclopaedias, dictionaries
(c) previous knowledge and experience of indexers, index-language compilers and users.

The more structured the source, or the more akin to a thesaurus in format, the more likely it is that the terms in the source will already be in a standard form ready for lifting wholesale and unmodified into a thesaurus. These sources which form the basis of the intellectual selection of terms may be augmented by or ousted by the machine selection of terms. Some or all of the terms in an index language may be derived automatically from the text of the documents to be indexed. Here again, the documents of the subject area, such as periodical articles, and research reports, will provide the terms to be included in the thesaurus.

3 *Record terms* In a totally computer-selected thesaurus, the listing of terms will be printed or displayed by the computer, and often no further effort is necessary. If the thesaurus includes humanly-selected terms, it is necessary to record the chosen terms. The most convenient manual format for recording terms is to write each term on a card, and to note on the card any comments about the term that are to feature in the thesaurus. Each card will show a term and any necessary scope notes, related terms and synonyms. For ease of consultation, cards should be kept in alphabetical order in accordance with the main term on the card. There are also computer-based systems which enable terms to be recorded as part of a thesaurus database. This thesaurus database may hold the terms, related terms, and notes concerning the terms. Terms may be added and sorted into alphabetical order. The choice between cards and a computer for thesaurus compilation depends upon a wide variety of factors, including:

● the anticipated size of the thesaurus
● the environment in which indexing is being conducted
● the availability of appropriate thesaurus-building software
● the purpose of the thesaurus in indexing and searching the database.

In general, with a small collection of data stored on cards, in printed form or in a small microcomputer-based database, cards are an appropriate medium for thesaurus compilation. If a large computer-based database is being compiled, then it is to be hoped that the software that is used to build the database has some facilities for assisting in the compilation (and later maintenance) of the thesaurus.

4   *Check relationships*   Most relationships indicated under each of the terms should be shown in both their direct and inverted form. Checks on relationships can be executed by examining each card in turn and seeking cards which show related terms. A more systematic approach involves assessing terms and their relationships in subject-related groups. These subject groups may be refined by constructing facets and hierarchies relevant to the subject under consideration. Graphic displays may also make a contribution here. Any new concepts or terms that arise during the relationship examination must also be inserted in the deck of cards.

5   *Finalize thesaurus*   Now is the time to conduct the final check on each of the features of the thesaurus. Terms should be reviewed for consistency and appropriate level of pre-coordination, word form and level of specificity. Classificatory or other indicators of relationships should be checked and recorded in their final form. If any links are necessary between displays and listings, some notation must be introduced. All listings for the final thesaurus must be converted to the format appropriate for typing, printing or input to a computer, and each feature, checked, edited, and tested on some examples. An introduction explaining the nature and scope of the thesaurus will enhance its value.

6   *Update thesaurus*   No indexing language is static. The thesaurus must be updated, whether new terms and relationships are added as and when necessary, or whether the thesaurus is reviewed at preset intervals. Updating an in-house thesaurus is relatively straightforward. Only a small number of existing versions of the thesaurus must be corrected. A published thesaurus may need to be amended by publishing a new edition. A thesaurus involved in an international cooperative scheme, such as that used in the International Road Research Documentation Scheme presents significant updating problems. Each amendment must be agreed by all participants, and equivalent terms in all of the languages of the thesaurus may need to be added. Machine-derived thesauri are not immune from the need for updating. These may be updated by the regular addition of terms after each new set of input is presented to the computer, or periodically at preset intervals. Any thesaurus will function adequately for only a limited period without revision.

Some of the more important features of controlled languages and their compilation have been reviewed in this chapter. Chapters 8 and 9 discuss some of the contexts in which such languages may be encountered.

6.8   The use of thesauri
The earlier sections of this chapter have described thesauri and their general purpose. This section examines a little more fully the way in which a thesaurus may be used.

The early thesauri were constructed for use with card-based post-coordinate indexing systems and with early computerized information-retrieval systems. These thesauri were typically printed (or typed) and were used alongside the index for which they were designed, to assist with both indexing and searching of the database. Printed thesauri are still important. For example, in conducting online searching of external databases, it is useful to have copies of printed thesauri relating to the index terms used in those database. Copies of these thesauri might also be available online and can be viewed at the terminal, but viewing the thesaurus at the terminal will take time and incur telecommunications and other charges, which would not be due if a printed thesaurus were consulted.

Many databases also have an online thesaurus. The availability of an online thesaurus depends on the availability of software to support such a facility. If the software package that is being used to create, maintain and search the database has the facility to build, maintain and exploit a thesaurus, then a thesaurus can be compiled and used to support both the indexing and the searching associated with the database. The thesaurus may contain natural-language terms that have been extracted from the records in the database, or controlled indexing-language terms that have been selected by the thesaurus designer. For more details of natural-language indexing and the use of go-lists and thesauri of natural-language terms, see Chapter 7.

A thesaurus of controlled-language indexing terms can be used in:

(a) the intellectual assignment of indexing terms to documents as their records enter the system. The permissible indexing terms and the relationship to other terms can be gleaned from a perusal of the thesaurus. On occasions, new terms will need to be added to the thesaurus and it will also be necessary to update the relationships between terms. Figure 6.3 shows two screens on thesauri in ADLIB-2; the top screen is for thesaurus maintenance, and the bottom for ROOT thesaurus display.

(b) searching of the database. Even a simple list of the terms that have been used to index records in the database can be a useful reference point for a searcher. A thesaurus which shows relationships between the terms in the thesaurus is a much more effective aid. The thesaurus may simple be available for the searcher to view, in order to offer inspiration in the selection of search terms. Other systems also employ a thesaurus in offering the facility to explode search profiles. Exploding, or automatically expanding, a search profile will cause the computer to retrieve all records indexed under related and synonymous terms, as well as those terms first specified by the user.

For example, in Henco's INFO, the command

RES *FLOWERS

searches for all occurrences of FLOWERS and its synonyms, if FLOWERS has been chosen as a synonym-group name.

Fig. 6.3   Thesaurus input screens in ADLIB-2

(a)   *Thesaurus maintenance screen*

```
                            Amend Relationships
                   Thesaurus Term Relationship Maintenance

Term: Special Usage Cements_____
Code: ABf_____
Relationship                                        Term

BT   hydraulic cements _____
NT   alumina cement _____
NT   barium cement_____
NT   low alkali cement_____
NT   polymer modified cement _____
NT   supersulphated cement _____
RT   portland cement _____
UF   magnesia cement _____

____ _____
____ _____

Enter term or press RETURN to exit
```

(b)   *ROOT thesaurus display screen*

```
ROOT THESAURUS REPORT

Computer software
  > computer programs
Computer storage devices
  < data media
Computer systems
  > computers
Computer technology
  – computer hardware
Computer terminals
  < computer peripheral equipment
  – modems
Computer typesetting
  = computer composition
Computer-oriented languages
  = assembly languages
  < programming languages
Computers
  = computer systems
  > analogue computers
  > hybrid computers
```

Reproduced with the permission of Databasix Ltd.

Appendix 6.1 Some extracts from thesauri

INSPEC thesaurus

(a) *A typical thesaurus entry*

database management systems

    UF databases
    NT relational databases
    BT file organisation
        management information systems
    TT computer applications
        file organisation
    RT database theory
        decision support systems
    CC C6160 C7100 C7250L
    DI   January 1977
    PT file organisation
        management information systems

TT= Top Term (in a hierarchy)
CC= Classification codes
DI= Date term was entered
PT= Prior terms, used in earlier indexing

(b) *Main alphabetical list*

DC machines
    UF direct current machines
    NT DC generators
    DC motors
       homopolar machines
    BT electric machines
    TT electric machines
    RT commutators
    CC B8320
    DI January 1985
    PT d.c. machines

DC motors
UF direct current motors
NT homopolar motors
BT DC machines
electric motors
TT electric machines
CC B8320
DI January 1985
PT d.c. motors

DC power transmission
UF direct current power transmission
BT power transmission
TT transmission
CC B8120G
DI January 1985
PT d.c. power transmission

DC sputter deposition
USE sputter deposition

DC sputtered coatings
USE sputtered coatings

(c) *Hierarchical list*

composite models of elementary particles
. composite models of hadrons
.. parton model
.. quark models
... colour model

composite particles
. alpha-particles
.. cosmic ray alpha-particles and helium nuclei
. deuterons
.. cosmic ray deuterons
. tritons

computation theory
. algorithm theory
.. computability
.. computational complexity
. automata theory
.. deterministic automata
.. finite automata
.. self-reproducing automata
.. sequential machines
.. stochastic automata
.. Turing machines
. computational linguistics
. formal logic
.. Boolean functions
.. computability
.. decidability
.. majority logic
.. many-valued logics
... ternary logic
.. probabilistic logic
.. recursive functions
.. threshold logic

ERIC Thesaurus

(a) *Main alphabetical list*

CUSTODIAN TRAINING   *Jul.1966*
     CIJE: 16   RIE: 30
BT   Job Training
RT   Job Skills
      School Maintenance

Cutaneous Sense (1968 1980)
USE   TACTUAL PERCEPTION

Cutlines
USE   CAPTIONS

CUTTING SCORES   *May. 1972*
      CIJE: 39   RIE: 496
SN   A selected point on a score scale
       which divides individuals earning
       scores above and below it into
       two groups for some purpose
UF   Critical Scores
BT   Scores
RT   Credit No Credit Grading
       Criterion Referenced Tests
       Equated Scores
       Mastery Tests
       Pass Fail Grading
       Raw Scores
       Scoring Formulas
       True Scores

Cyesis
USE   PREGNANCY

CYRILLIC ALPHABET   *Jul. 1966*
      CIJE: 6   RIE: 47
BT   Alphabets
RT   Slavonic Languages

CYTOLOGY   *Sep. 1968*
      CIJE: 80   RIE: 14
UF   Cell Theory (1966 1980)
BT   Biological Sciences
RT   Biochemistry
       Biology
       Culturing Techniques
       Embryology
       Evolution
       Physiology

CZECH   *Jul. 1966*
      CIJE: 11   RIE: 34
BT   Slavic Languages
RT   Czech Literature

Dactylology
USE   FINGER SPELLING

DAGUR   *Jul. 1966*
      CIJE: 0   RIE: 2
BT   Mongolian Languages

(b) *Descriptor groups*

Groups Related to LEARNING AND DEVELOPMENT

LEARNING AND PERCEPTION

Learning, conditioning and reinforcement; cognition and thought processes; and perception. *See also* MEASUREMENT, THE EDUCATIONAL PROCESS; CLASSROOM PERSPECTIVES, and DISABILITIES.

INDIVIDUAL DEVELOPMENT AND CHARACTERISTICS

Attributes of the individual, i.e., psychological characteristics, aptitudes, abilities, behavior, needs, and attitudes; growth and development; age groups; and individual differences. *See also* MENTAL HEALTH and THE INDIVIDUAL IN SOCIAL CONTEXT.

Groups Related to PHYSICAL AND MENTAL CONDITIONS

HEALTH AND SAFETY

Medicine and health, health conditions and services, and diseases; health occupations; health facilities; professional and paraprofessional health education; parts of the body; and accidents and safety. *See also* DISABILITIES.

(c) *Two-way hierarchical term display*

    : : : PUBLICATIONS
    : : REFERENCE MATERIALS
    : LIBRARY CATALOGS
    BOOK CATALOGS

    : : : ABILITY
    : : SKILLS
    : BUSINESS SKILLS
    BOOKKEEPING

: : : EQUIPMENT
: : MOTOR VEHICLES
: SERVICE VEHICLES
: : EQUIPMENT
: LIBRARY EQUIPMENT
BOOKMOBILES

: PUBLICATIONS
BOOK REVIEWS

: PUBLICATIONS
BOOKS
: FOREIGN LANGUAGE BOOKS
: HIGH INTEREST LOW VOCABULARY BOOKS
: PAPERBACK BOOKS
: TEXTBOOKS
: : HISTORY TEXTBOOKS
: : MULTICULTURAL TEXTBOOKS
: YEARBOOKS

: : : LIBERAL ARTS
: : : SCIENCES
: : NATURAL SCIENCES
: BIOLOGICAL SCIENCES
BOTANY

International road research documentation scheme thesaurus

(a) *Column from English alphabetical list*

       ELECTRIC CAR = ELECTRIC VEHICLE 12 82
       + CAR 12 43
1282 ELECTRIC VEHICLE
       ELECTRICAL CIRCUIT = CIRCUIT (ELECTR)
       6925
6946 ELECTRICAL INTERFERENCE
6954 ELECTRICITY
2121 ELECTROCARDIOGRAPHY
6951 ELECTRODE
2151 ELECTROENCEPHALOGRAPHY
7135 ELECTROLYSIS
       ELECTROLYTE = ELECTROLYSIS 7135
       ELECTRON = ELECTRONICS 6965

6965 **ELECTRONICS**
5785 **ELECTROOSMOSIS**
ELECTROPLATING = ELECTROLYSIS 7135
ELEPHANT FOOT ROLLER = SHEEPSFOOT
ROLLER 3695
ELEVATED HIGHWAY = BRIDGE 3455
ELEVATED ROAD = BRIDGE 3455
ELUTION = CHROMATOGRAPHY 7153
6221 **ELUTRIATION**
2801 **EMBANKMENT**
EMBEDMENT (PILE) = RESTRAINT (FIXING)
3422
2184 **EMERGENCY**
EMERGENCY STOPPING LANE = HARD
SHOULDER 2916
1261 **EMERGENCY VEHICLE** (*PREVIOUSLY 10 79*)
EMITTER = TRANSMITTER 6956
EMPIRICAL = TEST 6255
EMPLOYEE = PERSONNEL 0106
4995 **EMULSIFIER**
4993 **EMULSION**
4537 **ENAMEL**
5480 **ENERGY**

(b) *Column from numerical list*

3442 **COFFERDAM**
3448 **SKEW BRIDGE**
SKEW SLAB
3450 **CANTILEVER**
(SEGMENTAL CONSTRUCTION = BOX
GIRDER 34 74 + CANTILEVER 34 50)

3452 **SPAN**

3453 **GUSSET PLATE**

3455 **BRIDGE**
►ELEVATED HIGHWAY
►ELEVATED ROAD
►OVERPASS
►SKYWAY
►VIADUCT
►(TOLL BRIDGE = TOLL ROAD 27 02 +
BRIDGE 34 55)

3457 LIFTING BRIDGE
3458 TEMPORARY BRIDGE

3460 STIRRUP (REINFORCEMENT)
3461 BAR

3462 HINGE

3463 LATTICE
(VIERENDEEL = BEAM 34 72 +
LATTICE 34 63)
(WARREN = BEAM 34 72 + LATTICE
34 63)

(c) *Arrowgraph*

88

Chapter 7

NATURAL-LANGUAGE INDEXING

7.1 The nature of natural-language indexing

The focus of this text is abstracting and indexing as performed by people, even though we acknowledged in Chapter 1 that such indexing and abstracting may contribute to the compilation of a computer database. Since, in reality, natural-language indexing, i.e. indexing that relies upon the language of the document, is usually computer-assigned, it might be asserted that natural-language indexing is beyond the scope of this book. There remain, however, two sound reasons for including a brief chapter on natural-language indexing. These are:

1 to examine the merits and limitations of natural-language indexing, so that it is possible to judge when natural-language indexing is appropriate, and when controlled-language indexing is required. Controlled-language indexing is extremely time-consuming and costly and it would be uneconomic and foolish to persevere with human assignment of controlled-language terms, if the computer could be set to index a group of documents equally as, or even more, effectively than some human indexers.

2 to observe that in many real systems natural-language indexing and controlled-language indexing are applied side-by-side and, therefore, to explore more fully the context in which controlled-index language terms are exploited.

There is some debate as to the relative merits of controlled- and natural-language indexing. One school of thought holds that controlled-language indexing is the only 'proper' way to index, whilst others prefer to exploit to the full the opportunities offered by computer systems, even if the resulting index is less than perfect.

Natural-language indexing can be employed both in the searching of computer databases and in the production of printed indexes. One application of natural-language indexing is in the production of indexes based on words in titles, such as KWIC indexes. This application will be explored more fully in the next section. Consideration of the merits and limitations of such indexes provides a useful, concrete illustration of natural-language indexing in operation. Other topics that are relevant to natural-language indexing will be considered in other chapters in this book. For example, in Chapter 8, some of the retrieval facilities that are exploited in a post-coordinate indexing environment are more applicable if the search terms are drawn from a natural-indexing language, than if they are controlled-indexing terms. Chapter 9 cites many environments in which natural-language indexing is exploited. One of the objectives of this chapter is, then, to focus attention on natural indexing languages.

A first hurdle in discussing natural indexing languages is that it is not very easy to list them, or to identify what constitutes a natural indexing language. Certainly, traditionally, people did not produce lists of natural indexing languages. The indexing language is the language of the documents being indexed. Thus, a natural indexing language is only static as long as the document collection remains static. As soon as a new batch of documents is added to the system, the terms in the language change to accommodate any new terms in the new batch of documents. Clearly, with computer-based systems a list of the terms in the language at any point in time can normally be printed, so this would specify the indexing language. However, since each system indexes a separate set of documents, each system will have a different natural indexing language, even if the documents cover the same subject area. Furthermore, since the language is derived from the records input to the system, different records, even if they represent the same documents, may generate a different indexing language. Thus, abstracts, full text or citations, will generate different indexing languages. Clearly, great variations can be expected between different indexing languages for different databases. The characteristic feature of natural-language indexing is the absence of vocabulary control. This will permit the entire variety of natural language to be reflected in the indexing, and both the strengths and the weaknesses of natural-language indexing are founded on this basic characteristic.

7.2 Title indexes

Indexes based on the titles of documents were one of the first types of natural-language index. Title indexes are of two distinct types: those used simply as title indexes and those intended primarily as subject indexes. A conventional title index is merely an index of titles, with each title accompanied by a bibliographic reference, arranged in alphabetical order by the first word of the title. Many library catalogues and major bibliographies, such as the *British national bibliography*, include a title index to the documents listed. In this context subject and author sequences or indexes are usually also provided. Access is also often available via title in online public access catalogues. Sometimes this access offers retrieval on any word in the title, but in other systems retrieval is based on the first few characters or words in the title. The title index is thus an additional avenue of access to a document. Document details may be sought by using subject, author or title, depending upon which is known to the user. Such title indexes are relatively straightforward. It is the title index as a subject index on which we wish to focus attention.

A title indicates the subject content of a document. Thus, any index based upon document titles can help the user to assess the relevance of the works listed. Some indexes which are fundamentally a list of titles use arrangement of terms in the title to make them suitable for use as subject indexes under certain circumstances. Most such title indexes are computer-produced, although, in principle, they could be generated without the intervention of a computer. The previous chapter concentrated upon index languages and systems that involve intellectual assignment of index terms. Title indexes usually involve the machine selection of index terms from titles.

In some respects a title index is a poor substitute for a subject index. Problems arise from the limitations of titles as indicators of document content. In addition, absence of terminology control leads to various other problems. Title indexes then are not true subject indexes, and allowances should be made during searching.

Title indexes, despite their manifold weaknesses, have two important points in their favour which make them attractive for some library and information applications. Title indexes are both quick and cheap to prepare. Indexes are computer-generated merely by arrangement of a list of titles, with no human intervention. Standard program packages are readily available for the generation of some types of title index. In addition, many computerized information-storage and -retrieval system packages offer the facility for printing title indexes to the contents of a database.

7.3 KWIC indexes

KWIC, or Keyword-in-Context, indexes are a popular format for indexes to small to medium in-house collections and databases. KWIT indexes is merely another name for the same type of index. KWIT stands for Keyword-in-Title. Standard program packages are marketed which generate KWIC indexes, and several of the information-retrieval packages with a greater variety of outputs incorporate the facility for generating a KWIC index.

A simple KWIC index is, as the name suggests, based upon 'keywords' that appear in the titles of documents. All of the words in the titles of a batch of documents for which an index is required are matched, by a computer, against a stop-list. This stop-list or stop-wordlist is a record of words which have *no* currency as access points in an index. They convey, on their own, nothing of the subject content of a document but are included in the title as connectives or qualifiers. Words such as them, a, where, he, it, how, whether, are obvious candidates for inclusion in the stop-wordlist. Other words may be included in a stop-wordlist for some applications, but escape inclusion in other circumstances. Depending upon the subject orientation of the index, words such as machine, production, children, bolt, social sciences, may or may not be useful access points. Some words are useful only in particular circumstances because they take on a sufficiently precise meaning only in those contexts. Other words which might be feasible access points in a general index prove worthless in an index devoted to a special subject area because they appear in too high a proportion of the documents in the subject area to discriminate between subjects.

Index entries in a KWIC index are generated in association with all of the words in the batch of titles that are not stored in the stop-wordlist. In other words, all words in titles that are not found in the stop-wordlist for this particular system or index are regarded as keywords. Keywords are used as entry words with an entry being generated for every keyword. The word is printed and displayed 'in context', that is, together with the remainder of the title in which it appears. This 'context' includes any words previously designated as stop-words. Stop-words do not appear as entry words but they are displayed in the titles in the index. Entry words are arranged alphabetically (together with the remainder of the title) and printed in such a way that they are aligned in a centre or left-hand column. In this manner, a single line entry, which includes title and source reference of some type, is produced for each significant word or keyword in the title.

Consider the following titles:

● Welding the world's largest wire drums
● Wire rope lubrication and corrosion protection.

The first title would merit entries under each of the significant words. These would probably be judged to be: welding, wire, drums. The second title may be indexed under: wire, rope, lubrication, corrosion, protection. The words the, world's, largest, and, would probably be regarded as stop-words. An extract from a KWIC index is shown below. (Note the effect of truncation and wrap-around on clarity.)

ASITES/NEW CONCEPTS IN	FOODBOURNE ILLNESS BACTERIA VIRUS FUN	105266
ESSED CONDUCTION HEATED	FOODS/INST COMPUTER DETERMINATION O	105546
ID AND SUCCINIC-ACID IN	FOODS BY INST GAS CHROMATOGRAPHY BEE	102081
ERMINATION OF DULCIN IN	FOODS INST DIALYSIS/STUDIES ON DETE	102210
ON THE FLAVOURS USED IN	FOODS TYROPHAGUS-DIMIDIATUS YEAST IN	106332
ERMINATION OF DULCIN IN	FOODS 2 METHOD OF DETERMINATION OF D	102210
FROM INVESTIGATIONS ON	FOODSTUFF AND ARTICLES OF CONSUMPTION	102080
O RECEPTORS IN THE CATS	FOOT/THE NATURE AND LOCATION OF CER	103193

The source reference incorporated in a KWIC index is often no more than a document or abstract number. Abbreviated citations, showing perhaps an abbreviated journal title, volume and part numbers and page numbers are occasionally included if space permits. A full bibliographic citation, with or without abstract, can, if necessary, be provided in a separate listing. Alternatively, the document or abstract number may link the index user to entries in abstracts bulletins, or directly to a document in instances where the entire document collection is stored in accession or document number order.

7.4 Limitations of KWIC indexes

KWIC indexes have both advantages and disadvantages. On the plus side, KWIC indexes require a very low level of human effort or intervention in their production. The chief advantages of KWIC indexes are as follows:

1   A large number of titles can be processed quickly and cheaply.

2   Absence of interpretation of content leads to perfect consistency and predictability. If a word appears in the title of the document then it is certain that, unless the word is in the stop-wordlist, an entry will be generated under that word. There is no possibility, as there is with human indexers, of inconsistency in the allocation of terms. No scope for error or dispute exists.

3   The finished index will mirror current terminology. Words used as access points are those used by the author in his title. In as far as an author can be expected to be an expert in his field, the words used to describe the document should be both current and accurate. The correct inflection of meaning should be conveyed by the way in which the words are used in the title. However, this very aspect introduces an inconsistency. Successive indexes generated over a number of years will not be consistent in the terminology that they use. As a word drops out of vogue, the concept that it represents will, with time, gradually be described by a new term. An appreciation of the fashions in terminology in a given subject field will contribute to successful searching.

4   The cumulation of indexes is straightforward. Cumulation, provided that the complete index input is available, requires only an extra computer run. The computer will interfile the entries from a number of batches of input and print the cumulative index.

Despite their advantages KWIC indexes suffer from some severe limitations. Some of the features of KWIC indexes that have attracted criticism may be rectified moderately easily. Other characteristics must merely be recognized and allowances made during searching. KWIC indexes are imperfect because:

1   Titles do not always constitute an accurate summary of the content of a document. Some titles are deliberately misleading or eye-catching, rather than informative. Others are just plain contentless. For example, what conclusions about subject content can you draw from these two titles: 'How were you selected?', 'Integration: for and against: the case in favour'? There is some evidence to suggest that titles are becoming more informative, but titles will always be limited in the amount of information

that they can convey. A good title is by its very nature succinct. Some subjects simply cannot adequately be precisely specified by a short title. Further, any index based upon titles cannot hope to give access to all aspects of a document; only the main theme can normally be summarized in the title.

2   The simplest KWIC indexes are unattractive and tedious to scan owing to their physical format and typeface. Indexes are often printed on continuous computer stationery which is bulky and heavy. Lines printed on the stationery may cause eye-strain and line length for text may be longer than the eye can easily follow, without slipping to the next line. Despite this capacity for relatively long lines, there are usually some titles in any database or collection for which the allocated line length is not adequate. Titles which exceed the allocated line length will be truncated, possibly with the loss of valuable information as to content. Non-lined paper, the use of microform or photo-reduction, and increased line length can reduce the drawbacks of poor physical format. The typefaces available for computer print-out may detract from the scannability of an index. Although the range of typefaces generally available has improved over the past few years, some KWIC indexes are still printed entirely in upper case. Upper case can be more tiring to scan than text displayed in both upper and lower case. Keywords can prove difficult to identify immediately and their alphabetical sequence can be less than straightforward to follow. The nature of the display may lead to truncation of the title and make the title awkward to read in the proper sequence.

3   Long sequences of entries under one keyword appear to be almost inevitable at some place in an index. Several pages of entries under one keyword are very discouraging, especially if the titles give insufficient information for some documents to be rapidly rejected. Sub-arrangement at entry terms can break down long sequences of entries listed under the same keyword. Various means of improving upon the normal alphabetical sub-arrangement, which is dictated by the accident of the order of terms in the title, have been tried. These are mentioned in the next section.

4   Title indexes have always been plagued by the absence of terminology control. Terminology control is the objective of a controlled-indexing-language system. The user of such indexes can expect some consistency in the use of index terms to describe any given concept, and some guidance concerning related index terms which might also be consulted. With machine-assigned indexing irrelevant and redundant entries are inevitable. The appearance of a term in a title does not necessarily herald the treatment of the topic at any length in the body of the text. Equally important, a word may not convey the author's intended meaning unless the word can be taken in context. Lack of terminology control will lead to similar subjects being scattered under different terms. No guidance will be given as to which alternative terms

should also be sought. The KWIC index user will profit from an insight into the terminology of the subject area, either together with, or instead of, a list, thesaurus or dictionary of words showing related or synonymous terms. Searching for related subjects, in order to narrow or broaden a search also presents problems since no recognized hierarchical structure is incorporated into the index. Locating documents on concepts that must be described by a string of words, such as those subjects catered for by pre- and post-coordinate indexes, is far from straightforward in a title index. Such documents can be retrieved only by scanning all of the titles listed under one of the words which describes part of the concept.

7.5 Further title indexes and their variants

Simple KWIC indexes are an admirable solution to the rapid and cheap generation of a retrieval tool to a collection of documents. But KWIC indexes require special skill to search effectively, and, hence, their use should be restricted primarily to those situations where the index will be consulted only by information or subject specialists. Some of their drawbacks make regular use rather tiresome. Taking into account both indexing and searching effort a KWIC index is most appropriate for an index that will be studied only infrequently.

It is relatively easy to improve upon the readability of a KWIC index. Various printed formats have been tried for title indexes. A KWOC (Keyword-Out-of-Context) index, for instance, is a title index where the keywords are extracted from the titles and displayed as a heading. Titles and reference numbers are displayed beneath the keywords. One entry is generated for each significant keyword in a title. In a true KWOC index an asterisk appears in the printed title in the position of and instead of the keyword that features as heading. Indexes where the keyword appears both as heading and again in the title are strictly KWAC indexes (Keyword-and-Context). However, the distinction between KWOC and KWAC indexes is rarely made and KWOC is the generic term that is usually used. Superficially, KWOC indexes appear to be conventional subject indexes. Particular attention should be paid to discriminating between KWOC indexes and a subject index based on assigned terms. A KWOC index should be searched very differently. The tell-tale signs that mark a KWOC index include:

(a) in a KWOC index all of the words that appear as headings have been extracted from titles

(b) in a KWOC index some of the headings are unqualified adjectives, e.g. handicapped, circular, since all headings are usually one-word terms.

Shown below is an example of a KWOC index format.

ADULTS
A DESCRIPTIVE STUDY OF BLACK AMERICAN   *   OF ACHIEVEMENT FROM AN EXISTENTIAL
   FRAMEWORK.   097861
A STUDY OF THE VISUAL LANGUAGE PROCESSING ABILITIES OF BRAIN INJURED   *   :APRAXIC
   VERSUS DYSARTHRIC SUBJECTS   097865
VISUAL SEQUENTIAL RECALL OF ASSOCIATIVE AND NON-ASSOCIATIVE STIMULI IN UNILATERALLY
   BRAIN-DAMAGED AND NORMAL   *   067524

ADVANCED
THE   *   EVOLUTION OF GLOBULAR CLUSTER STARS   045879

ADVANTAGE
THE RIGHT EAR * FOR THE PROCESSING OF LINGUISTIC STIMULI   067890

Simple re-formatting of the display in an index can provide only limited improvements. One of the problems that remains is the almost inevitable long lists of entries under one term. Sub-arrangement under an entry term can alleviate the onerous task of scanning long lists of entries under the same keyword. Normally, entries under one keyword are alphabetically arranged by accident of whichever word happens to occur next to the keyword in the title. If entries are arranged alphabetically by a significant qualifying term (i.e. one of the other keywords) the index user is relieved of the necessity of scanning every entry under a term. Only those entries that feature the appropriate qualifying term need be examined. The solution is fine when the qualifying term that the user seeks is present, and is used relatively consistently. But when the term that the user expects to find as the qualifying term is not used by the author in his title the user must invent alternative qualifiers and search under these. If the user cannot imagine alternative qualifying terms he may have to resort to scanning the entire list of entries under the first keyword. In indexes with sub-arrangement the number of entries under one index heading or keyword will, in general, be longer than in a simple KWIC index.

The Double-KWIC index is a common type of title index that incorporates sub-arrangement at entry terms. We will examine the entries for the first significant keyword in the title first. This keyword is extracted from the title and regarded as the main index heading or ordering device. The position from which the keyword was drawn is occupied by an asterisk. The remaining words in the title are rotated, using a wrap-around format, in such a matter that each of the other keywords appears, in turn, as the second element after the main term. This procedure is responsible for generating not one, but several entries for each document under any of the keywords in the title, as the procedure will be repeated and applied to each of the keywords in a title by turn. Index entries are ordered alphabetically by main term, and within groups of entries under one main term, alphabetically by secondary or sub-term. Double-KWIC indexes come into their own with concepts that are best described by two words. Apart from this additional facility Double-KWIC indexes have most of the facilities, features and drawbacks of KWIC and KWOC indexes.

96

The Permuterm index (as featured in Science, and Social Sciences Citation Indexes) is similar to a Double-KWIC index in that it provides for simple coordination of index words. Actual titles are not displayed, but the words which form the basis of the index entries are extracted from titles. Pairs of keywords are extracted from each title to be indexed; these form the components of the index entries. Each entry consists of two words. Each keyword is displayed in juxtaposition to each of the other keywords that appear in the same title. Main entry points are arranged alphabetically, and sub-terms are filed alphabetically within the set of entries under each main term. An accession number accompanies each pair of keywords, but no titles are included in the index. This serial or accession number can be used to access titles in a separate listing. An abbreviated citation might serve the same function or permit direct retrieval of the document. A Permuterm index scores over a Double-KWIC index in that it avoids repetitive printing of one title. Also the entries are shorter, and the entire index occupies less space than a Double-KWIC index. However, a Double-KWIC index offers the user additional data upon which to base any relevance assessment, and may make selection of relevant documents speedier. Some entries in a Permuterm-type index are shown below.

MAN		MENTAL	648
CLINICAL	506	STOMACH	534
COLLAPSE	583	VOICE	498
DEATH	671	**MENTAL**	
DIABETIC	591	CAPACITY	487
DRUNKARD	591	HEALTH	584
EPILEPTIC	591	MAN	648
EXCUSE	506	NURSE	615
EXEMPTION	701	NURSING	615
FOOD	693	PSYCHOLOGY	617
HEART	583		

The quality of machine indexing can be enhanced by widening the indexing field. The computer may be provided with more text than merely the title from which to make a selection of index terms or, alternatively, some human intervention in the assignment of index terms may be introduced. There are many indexes based primarily, but not solely, upon titles; the keywords in the title are augmented by additional assigned keywords which are treated in the same way as the keywords in the title. A number of options are available.

1 Terms intended for use as index terms may be added to the title, merely by placing them at the end of the title. If these terms are input with the titles to which they pertain the additional words will be treated just as if they were part of the title proper. These additional terms can

contribute to making indexing more exhaustive and more specific, and can be used to eliminate the problems of uninformative or misleading titles. But the skills of a human indexer must be called upon for the assignment of these additional terms. Extra or supplementary index terms may be part of a free or controlled vocabulary. If terms are drawn from a controlled vocabulary the selection of index headings no longer depends entirely upon the whim of the author in framing a title. The searcher can expect that there is a greater likelihood of all documents on a subject being collected under the same index heading. These terms are known to be assigned because they reflect subject content, and not merely because they happen to feature in a title. However, because of the continued presence of terms selected automatically from titles, the mixture of humanly-assigned and machine-assigned terms can confuse the searcher.

2   All keywords or potential keywords in titles may be designated manually prior to input. A recognized character, e.g. @, prefaces each keyword. Obviously, this tagging must be conducted manually, but tagging involves less evaluation and assessment than true intellectual indexing. The chief gain from tagging is that terms are selected as entry points in accordance with their applicability to a certain document, and not merely because they happen to appear in a title. More minor concepts which receive only scant attention in a document will not be responsible for creating index entries whether they are mentioned in the title or not. Tagging also caters well for multiple-word concepts. Index terms comprising several words may be tagged as one term, and the words retained as a linked unit. Subject areas that abound in multiple-word concepts benefit from tagging.

3   A go-list or comparison thesaurus extends the control exercised over the terms that are acceptable indexing terms, without having to resort to human intervention for every individual document. Also, the predictability of computer indexing is retained. The vocabulary used in such systems is controlled in the sense that the go-list specifies those terms that are permitted as index terms. The use, however, of the vocabulary is not controlled. If a word or term appears in both a title and the go-list then automatic indexing occurs under that term. Text as a basis for the selection of index tems is normally matched against both stop-lists and go-lists. As usual, the presence of a term in a title and the stop-list will definitely cause an entry not to be created. The presence of other terms in the go-list and a title will positively cause an entry to be recorded. Any words appearing in titles but not already included in either the go-list or stop-list must be printed or displayed for indexer consideration. Usually the indexer will then assign words previously unknown to the system to either the go-list or the stop-list.

4   Editing the input to a KWIC program with the object of controlling subject scatter can make the resultant index easier to use. Trivial words

can be suppressed, inconsistent spellings, abbreviations, word variants and multiple-word terms can be handled at the input stage.

5   Cross references may be incorporated into an index. These cross references must be inserted as a separate operation. In a KWIC index they would be standard references that appeared with only minor modifications in each edition of the index. Cross references that prove helpful will be between related terms, where each of the connected pair of terms is known to occur frequently in the titles of the literature of the subject.

6   Very much more sophisticated indexing systems can be evolved if the field from which terms are selected is expanded beyond the title and a few supplementary terms. Terms may be selected from abstracts and/or full text, as well as from the title. Such broad selection may also warrant the use of go- and stop-lists. This solution is discussed in the following section.

7.6 Natural-language indexing on abstracts and full text
Clearly, natural-language indexing on titles is restricted, but a study of the problems encountered in indexing on words in titles can form a good basis for examining natural-language indexing on abstracts and full text. As with words in titles, it is possible to use other words in other parts of the record as search keys. Clearly, the words that can be used depend on the structure of the record. In order to be able to search on words in abstracts, or the full text of a document, there must be fields present in the record which contain these items. There are, however, three fundamental differences between indexing on words in titles and words in longer documents or records. These are:

(a)   The number of potential indexing words is very much greater in longer documents or records and is, indeed, related to the length of the record.

(b)   Due to their greater number the variety of index words is greater, and words are more likely to appear that have not necessarily been selected as representative of the document content.

(c)   Much of the foregoing discussion on title indexes has focused on printed indexes. Words in titles can also be used to search databases online. Words in abstracts and full text of documents are used almost entirely to search databases on a computer system.

Natural-language indexing is exemplified in many systems either by the use of a character-string search which is a serial search on part of the file, or by the creation of inverted files on fields containing natural-language terms. Typically, inverted files will be constructed of search keys, which will provide inverted files for fields such as index terms, authors' names, journal titles, classification codes, etc. Most of these fields will comprise controlled indexing terms, but some may contain natural-language terms. Terms in these fields can then be quickly retrieved with the aid of the inverted file. The inverted file provides direct access to records with those search keys included in them. Other terms that are not included in the index can be located within a record, or used as a search key, only by searching serially through the file. Normally, it is uneconomic and very time-consuming to perform a serial search of a large file, so that serial searching for a string of characters is usually performed on a small subset of the file. This subset will usually have been previously identified by a search on indexed fields. For example, if we are interested in documents on Greenhouses, but Greenhouses is not a term in the controlled indexing vocabulary used with the database, then we might search under Glasshouses (which is listed in the database's thesaurus) instead, and retrieve a set of documents that had the controlled index-language term Glasshouse assigned and, then, perform a string search on the term 'Greenhouses' to discover whether this term appeared in the text of any of the records retrieved by the first search. This is a typical example of the way in which searching on natural-language terms can be used in conjunction with searching on controlled index terms to yield maximum retrieval for as many users as possible.

Most information-retrieval systems are based on special-purpose text- or information-retrieval software which runs on general-purpose computers. A few special-purpose computers, or hardware-based information-retrieval systems are beginning to enter the market. Hypersearch is an external search-processor developed by Memex Information Engines Ltd for Gould Electronics Power-Node 6000 and 9000 series computers. Hypersearch does not require indexes of fields in the record but, rather, performs a very fast serial search of the complete database when a search request is submitted. Such systems, then, whilst they can search on controlled indexing terms, are specifically geared towards searching of natural-language terms.

Stop-lists and Go-lists
Stop-lists and go-lists have already been mentioned earlier in this chapter when discussing title indexes. Such devices do have particular merits in controlling the entries that appear in a printed index. They can also be employed to restrict the number of entries listed in inverted files. In particular, if an inverted file of a natural-language field, say, the title field, is created, a stop-list can be employed to prevent terms of no significance in retrieval being listed in the inverted file. This will reduce the size of the inverted file.

In natural-language indexing which uses a stop-list only, the indexing language is open, and there is no record other than the index itself of the indexing terms that have been assigned. The indexing changes gradually with time, as the natural language of the documents that the index covers evolves.

The other approach to natural-language indexing is to index on both a stop-list and a go-list. A go-list includes all of those terms that would create useful index entries in the subject area being indexed. Thus, the go-list must be machine-stored and is used by the computer in the assignment of index terms. Like the stop-list, the go-list can also be displayed or printed out for consideration prior to updating or other modification. The go-list is sometimes known as a thesaurus and, indeed, is a form of natural-language thesaurus. In the process of indexing each new batch of documents, new words will from time to time appear in the text. Since these words are new they will not appear in the go-list and the computer will not know whether or not to treat them as indexing terms. In this case, the human indexer will be provided with the terms not recognized by the computer, and must decide whether to list them in the go-list or the stop-list or, perhaps, to leave them unlisted in either list, so that they will be output for human indexer consideration on each occurrence. Obviously, this last option permits the human indexer some control over the allocation of index terms. Perhaps it is useful to observe that the human indexer selects the terms for inclusion in the go-list, and in that sense the indexing language is controlled. However, the allocation of index terms, and the variety of forms in which concepts or names might appear, is not controlled.

Neither stop-lists or go-lists are relevant to string-searching where a serial search of natural-language terms is performed.

To pursue the parallels between printed title indexes and online searching of natural-language terms further, it is useful to summarize the attractions and limitations of natural-language indexing, and then proceed to list some examples of circumstances in which natural-language indexing is particularly valuable.

7.7 Attractions of natural-language indexing

The attractions of natural-language indexing may be divided into two categories:

1 *Economic factors* The intellectual input at the indexing stage is minimal, even in systems where in the interests of enhanced consistency there is some intervention at the indexing stage. Indexing can thus be achieved at a detailed level, with often many terms per document, with almost no indexing effort. The effort must be input in another way. Effective retrieval from natural-language indexed databases requires sophisticated search software. The user must become familiar with the facilities of this search software and, therefore, may need more training than might be necessary for the retrieval of information in a database which has been indexed with a controlled indexing language. For example,

search software offers the type of facilities discussed in Chapter 8, including the ability to search on words in predetermined fields, the ability to search on word stems and to search on words with variant spellings and, then, the ability to rank the retrieved material according to its relative significance.

2 *Language factors* In some circumstances natural-language indexing may reflect more closely the terms used by the searcher. For instance, if the searcher seeks documents on Chalets and this is not an index term in the appropriate controlled indexing language, then documents on this topic will be difficult to retrieve directly. Also, in controlled-indexing-language databases, there is often an assumption that a user will be prepared to chase strings of references, or to consult a, sometimes, complex thesaurus. This may not always be the case.

The other problems that sometimes occur in controlled-language indexing which are avoided by natural-language indexing, arise from the limitations of the human mind. Human indexers sometimes make inappropriate judgements, misinterpret ideas, have lapses of memory or concentration, and generate omissions and inconsistencies in their indexing.

7.8 Problems with natural-language indexing

Indexers nave used controlled-language indexing and authority lists of standard forms of terms and names for many years. These practices have emerged from the fact that natural-language indexing is often not adequate, for one or more of the following reasons:

(a) *Semantics*, including synonyms, variant word forms, antonyms, etc. The user must consider all of the possibilities. In this he may be assisted by the opportunity to use truncation, alphabetical lists of terms showing word variants, etc.

(b) *Homographs*, and words where the meaning is context dependent. Terms with more than one meaning, e.g. intelligence, which means either an individual's analytical and reasoning abilities or information on an adversary, must be recognized by the searcher to have possible dual meaning. Contextual logic may help in the elimination of unwanted uses of the homograph.

(c) *Hierarchical and other relationships* No cross references can be expected. Retrieval of documents on a search topic, but using the terms for a broader or narrower concept, relies heavily upon the searcher's ingenuity, and any additional relationships that the database indexer might have added to link the natural-language index terms.

7.9 Circumstances in which natural-language indexing is particularly appropriate

1 Searches that predominantly involve specific words or phrases known to have been used in the source material. Obvious examples are the unique proper nouns such as brand names and company names, although there can be problems with:

- company names that may be in full or abbreviated, e.g. DEC, Digital Equipment
- company names that may appear with or without a hyphen, e.g. Perkin Elmer, Perkin-Elmer
- brand names that consist of common words, e.g. Crest, Tube Investments
- companies known by two or more names, e.g. GPO, British Telecom.

Most of these problems can be overcome, with the use of Boolean and contextual logic.

2 Slogans, quotations and catch phrases, which may or may not be indexed under a controlled indexing language, e.g. inter-racial adoption.

3 Geographic names can be very direct labels, but there are a number of well-known problems with geographic names. These include:

- place names which recur in different states and countries, e.g. Berlin, in New Hampshire and Germany
- vague place names, e.g. Tyneside, the Peak District
- different levels of specificity, e.g. West Midlands, Birmingham, Midlands.

To overcome these problems users must think of all the various names that might have been applied, and must understand something of the geography and administration of the locality concerned. A further problem is the fact that place names may appear in a trivial context. For example, a headline announcing 'Mrs Thatcher at Oxford hears of second Falkland crisis' does not merit retrieval under Oxford, but does require to be retrieved under Falkland.

In conclusion, natural language indexing has its strengths and weaknesses, but will certainly continue to be used as part of the retrieval armory in computer-based information systems.

Chapter 8

POST-COORDINATE INDEXING SYSTEMS

8.1 Principles

Post-coordinate indexes were conceived by Mortimer Taube in the early
1950s, as a means of dealing with the research reports acquired by the
US Armed Services Technical Information Agency. Although the concepts
and applications of post-coordinate indexing have evolved considerably
since the 1950s, the essence of a post-coordinate indexing system remains
constant. Taube's original system relied upon 'uniterms' or one-concept
terms. Each document to be indexed was first assigned some type of
accession number or serial number, and was then analysed and its subject
represented by a number, perhaps 10 or 20, of one-concept terms. The
accession number pertaining to a given document was then entered under
each of these index terms. The searcher compares entries under several
index terms in order to retrieve document numbers for documents that
cover the specific subjects represented by a combination of index terms.
The essential feature of a post-coordinate indexing system is that concepts
are coordinated at the search stage, i.e. a number of headings are searched
in such a way that document numbers assigned to more than one term
in the combination can be selected. A post-coordinate index depends upon
specialized equipment and storage devices. Taube's indexes were based
upon 'uniterm cards' (see below), a card-based system, but the indexing
principles of this system have been adapted and further evolved in
computer-based information-retrieval systems.

Since the card-based systems in which post-coordinate indexing was
first conceived are more-or-less redundant, the newcomer to the subject
may be forgiven for concluding that the concept of post-coordinate indexing is dead. Nothing could be further from the truth. Computer-based
systems offer such great opportunities for coordination of index terms
during the search process that, increasingly, information-retrieval systems
use some form of post-coordinate indexing. An understanding of the
common principles of a post-coordinate index, whether it be card-based
or computer-based, is an important prerequisite to successful retrieval.

8.2 Computerized databases v. cards in post-coordinate index systems

The first post-coordinate indexing systems were based on various different kinds of cards and other lists. These have now been largely superseded as retrieval systems by the indexes and retrieval systems associated with computer-based databases. The retrieval facilities offered in such environments depend upon the nature of the database (e.g. indexing terms included, fields in records) and upon the software that is used to create, maintain and retrieve information from the database.

Computerized systems offer a wide range of potential search strategies and searching aids. Also, computerized systems make search strategies that are possible but tedious with card-based systems more straightforward and possibly more effective. Computerized systems have more options for searching specific subjects and topics that need to be described by a complex string of terms.

Why have card-based systems been overtaken by computer databases? Most card-based systems have a limited capacity, either in terms of the number of documents that can be indexed under the system, or in terms of the number of index terms that can be admitted to the system, or both. This restricted capacity means that card-based systems are more suited to circumstances where the index caters for a specialized and narrow subject area or a small self-contained collection of documents or information. Thus, card-based post-coordinate indexes primarily found application in special libraries including industrial libraries, art libraries, and research and government libraries, and in special collections in larger libraries. The physical format of card-based post-coordinate indexes also restricts their use to sectors in which the librarian or information officer acts as an intermediary between the index and its users. Card-based post-coordinate indexes are not amenable to searching by the library's clientele; their effective operation is not immediately obvious to the uninitiated and the cards in the index are liable to become disorganized if inexperienced information-seekers tamper with the index.

Computer-based systems have largely ousted card-based systems. As mini- and micro-computers become cheaper and information-retrieval software becomes available in more financially attractive, user friendly and tried and tested packages, the trend towards local computerized information-retrieval systems is likely to be reinforced. Furthermore, in due course, some of these systems will be linked to large online systems and networks. Computerized information-retrieval systems which incorporate some of the principles of post-coordinate indexing are not only evident in special collections and special indexes, they are also very prominent in commercially available online search systems and applications. Systems such as Dialog, IRS (Information Retrieval Service), Pergamon's ORBIT and the British Library's BLAISE, may be accessed by libraries and information units. They all permit an element of coordination of concepts at the search stage when searching most of the databases that are on offer.

Card-based post-coordinate indexing systems were associated with controlled indexing languages. The terms in the controlled indexing language were normally recorded in a thesaurus, which indicated preferred and non-preferred terms, and the relationships between those terms. Several terms were assigned for each document. Terms were brought together or coordinated during the search by making selections of appropriate groups of cards. Various retrieval facilities, such as Boolean logic operators, were used in this environment. In computer-based systems, the terms which are used as search keys may be:

- terms from a controlled indexing language, such as might be recorded in a thesaurus. These terms may be computer-assigned or humanly-assigned
- terms from the text of the record.

The first of these categories is very similar in principle to the card-based post-coordinate indexing systems, but the second does not involve indexing by humans. The computer effectively assigns the terms, and the only role of people is in searching. It becomes all the more imperative to consider indexing and searching as two linked facets.

All post-coordinate indexing systems have the following three features which may make their use without any degree of coordination very tedious:

(a) None of the entries in the system is specific. There is a relatively large number of documents under each heading, and if the searcher approaches the index as a conventional index he is liable to become involved in extensive scanning of the many entries under each heading in order to discriminate between relevant and less relevant documents.

(b) There is usually a larger number of entries in a post-coordinate indexing system than in an index based upon pre-coordinate indexing principles, although the number of entries in a pre-coordinate system will depend upon the incidence of references and multiple entries.

(c) The number of different headings in the index is relatively small because, as in classification, a synthetic scheme needs fewer categories or headings than an equivalent enumerative scheme.

Traditionally, post-coordinate indexing systems can be grouped into two main categories: those systems or indexes based on 'item records' and those using 'term records' as their fundamental unit. An 'item-record file' is a file in which records are serially ordered by document identifier or number. Each entry or record stores the total information relating to one document that is available in the system, including reference and index terms. A 'term-record file', conversely, is a file that is ordered by index terms, with each entry an index term and the document representations listed in association with that term.

8.3 Card-based indexes

The more detailed consideration of post-coordinate indexing systems starts with a brief outline of some card-based indexes. This description has historical value, but is also an effective means of conveying the basic concepts of post-coordinate indexing. Card-based indexes can be divided into item-record indexes and term-record indexes.

An item-record post-coordinate index may take one of several physical forms. The physical form imposes limitations upon the type of information or data that may be stored and the way in which the index can be searched.

1 *A list of terms* on the cover or front page of the documents to be indexed constitutes the simplest form of item-record index. Plainly, this is not a very satisfactory type of index because in order to search the index the entire list of index terms assigned to each of the documents must be scanned in order to retrieve those documents with the desired combination of index terms.

2 *Catalogue cards*, with each card representing one document and the terms and citation of a document listed on that card, are a minor improvement over the first option above.

3 *Marginal storage cards* or edge notch cards are probably the commonest form of non-computerized item-record index. Each card acts as a surrogate for one document, and the index terms for that document are encoded around the edge of the card. Edge notch cards have a series of holes around their perimeter, and the piece of card between the hole and the edge of the card may be removed, using a punch, to form a notch. The pattern of notches and holes along the edge of a card stores the index terms assigned to the document for which the card is acting as surrogate. Searching is performed by inserting a needle through the whole pack of cards at the position of the hole(s) which represent the terms to be searched. The notched cards, representing relevant documents, will drop off the needle and fall from the bulk of the pack. The term 'false drops' which is encountered in other aspects of information retrieval can trace its pedigree to edge notch cards. False drops are cards which drop from the needle when the documents that the cards represent are not truly relevant to the topic of a search.

To take an example of needling the pack, suppose that in an index covering Education it is necessary to identify all of the documents indexed under the term 'Secondary schools'. If 'Secondary schools' is a term in the indexing language used in the index this might be coded and represented by a hole numbered '8'. When a needle is inserted through the '8' position all cards in the pack with the hole '8' notched out will drop from the needle. Thus, all cards corresponding to documents covering 'Secondary schools' are withdrawn from the pack.

4 *Aperture cards* are a special form of marginal store card which permit the entire document to be stored in the centre of the card. A microform insert which contains the full text of the document being indexed is attached to the centre of the card. An index using aperture cards is more than an index, it is a complete document collection, and cards must be withdrawn in order to read documents. The reader is left to debate the relative merits of such a format—obviously its applications are limited. Aperture cards are the standard form for storing technical drawings and have been used in connection with patents. Documents may be retrieved by means of the coding around the edge of the card, and apart from the microfiche insert are similar to other marginal storage cards.

Term-record card indexes also emerge in a number of different physical guises:

1 *Term cards* are the simplest format that can be adopted in a term-record index. An index based on term cards appears superficially little different from an ordinary card index, although in searching it must be noted that the index is in fact a post-coordinate index. Each index term claims one card in the index, and on that card are displayed document numbers or very brief references to those documents for which the particular index term has been assigned.

2 *Terminal digit cards* are a special type of term card. Sometimes known as term cards, terminal digit cards have the document numbers listed on each card arranged in an order which is designed to facilitate scanning and comparison of lists of numbers. Each document number is entered in the column of the card according to its terminal or last digit. Thus, each card is divided into ten vertical columns headed, respectively, from 0 to 9.

3 *Dual dictionaries* can most plainly be described as computer-produced 'term cards'. Usually two identical lists are printed on continuous computer stationery. In each list index terms are arranged alphabetically, and document numbers are listed under each index term. Numbers may be grouped in columns as in terminal digit cards. Searches are executed by comparing visually the numbers entered under two or more index terms. The chief merit of a dual dictionary as a format for a post-coordinate index is that a dual dictionary, as distinct from card-based indexes, can be reproduced in multiple copies.

4 *Optical coincidence cards* are one of the more popular physical formats for a post-coordinate index. Such cards, alternatively known as Peek-a-boo or Batten cards, are available in various sizes and styles. They all have space at the top for a keyword and the index is arranged in alphabetical order by keyword. Each card has a grid covering most of

the body of the card which provides for the coding of document numbers. When a document number is to be stored on the card pertaining to a given index term a hole is punched in the position that serves to represent that number. Searching involves reading the coding corresponding to the position of the holes, and comparing the holes that recur on more than one card, by 'optical coincidence'. Cards are superimposed, one on top of another, and carefully aligned. Examination reveals positions on the cards where the light passes through all of the cards in a stack. These positions correspond to documents that have been indexed under each of the index terms whose cards have been selected from the index and compared.

Optical coincidence cards are usually stored in a tray which displays the index terms at the top of each card in such a way that the alphabetical sequence can be readily followed and interesting cards can be withdrawn easily. Optical coincidence cards have been one of the more common formats for post-coordinate indexes, and they have achieved this status because they have the potential to store a relatively large number of documents; larger cards have 9,999 coding positions, and can thus store 9,999 document numbers, or represent the indexing of 9,999 documents.

5 *Edge punch cards* have already been considered as a basis for an item-record index; they may also be used in a term-record index. In this application, each card contains all of the data relating to a given index term. The coding positions around the periphery of the card are punched in order to represent the numbers of the documents indexed under a specific index term.

8.4 Retrieval in a post-coordinate index

Output

The output from a post-coordinate index depends both on the input to the system, and the physical nature of the store. Different stores offer access to distinct types of information or data and permit the information to be manipulated to varying extents. Some possible levels of access are:

(a) store provides a reference or document number
(b) store allows direct retrieval of data or information (as in legal and statistical computer-held data banks and some other item-record indexes)
(c) store permits the manipulation of data after they have been selected and retrieved, but both the outcome of the manipulations and the original data are available from the store
(d) store permits the processing of the information that it contains, but, after processing, the data in the store differ from the initial content (for example, in the editing and amending of catalogue records).

Some computerized indexing systems may offer any of the four levels of access, although other post-coordinate indexing systems operate at only one or two levels of access. In other words, the output from a post-coordinate index is generally in the form of document numbers and/or references, or the document itself.

Searching an index is the process of scanning the index records to determine which identifiers are associated with a certain search key or combination of keys or index terms. In this context the records that are selected for perusal and as being potentially relevant depend upon the quality of indexing in the system and the skills of the searcher. The quality of indexing is influenced by:

- the quality of the thesaurus
- the standard of indexing, e.g. thoroughness, consistency
- the complexity of the relationships between concepts present in the search statement
- the intellectual level and intent of document content in the subject area
- the audience orientation of both the original documents and their indexing
- the quality of the document and its associated record, e.g. content, style of presentation
- the nature of the document, e.g. whether tables, diagrams and illustrations are used.

A full information search extends to more than one index and the success or otherwise of the search does not depend entirely upon the merits or otherwise of one index. The skilled searcher knows not only how to search individual indexes, but also which sources to tap first, and can often take shortcuts by heading straight for the most effective index for his purposes. Humans conduct iterative searching: that is, they modify their search strategy as the search progresses. Unfruitful lines of enquiry are dropped and new and more promising search tems are introduced as the search progresses. It is important that a post-coordinate index should offer the facility for the modification of search strategy. Computers, on the other hand, adhere to their initial instructions and execute these relentlessly until the task that is set is completed. A computer search will explore every avenue in a network of cross references in a manner that would prove both exhausting and time-consuming if pursued in a manual search. The quality and appropriateness of the end product of a search depends upon the recognition of these factors.

Search logic
One of the characteristic features of a post-coordinate indexing system is that searching amounts to more than making a note of the records listed

under one index heading. Post-coordinate indexes are expected to be searched by comparing records entered in association with two or more index headings or terms. Indeed, some questions which start with only two or three terms may, after full consideration of all alternative and related terms, involve many more. Because of the connections between the terms and the roles of the various terms in specifying the question, not all terms are necessarily required to be assigned to a document for the document to be considered to be pertinent. Search logic is the means of specifying the acceptable combinations of terms which when assigned to a document cause it to be assessed as relevant. Various logic devices have been tried, and the possibilities for more sophisticated logical statements are greatly enhanced in computer-based systems. The next section will proceed to consider some logic operators and devices for making logical statements. Remember, nevertheless, that although post-coordinate indexes are preoccupied with the coordination of concepts, single-concept searches are still possible. For an example, see figure 8.1.

Boolean search logic
Boolean logic is the logic system employed in searching most post-coordinate indexes. The logic is used to link the terms which describe the concepts present in the statement of the search. As many as 20, 30 or more index terms may be linked together with search logic in order to frame the search profile. Search logic permits the inclusion of all synonyms and related terms, and also specifies acceptable and unacceptable term combinations. The Boolean logic operators are AND, OR and NOT. Figure 8.2 uses Venn diagrams to help explain how each of these operators may be used. The sets of documents indexed under the two index terms A and B are each represented by a circle.

Boolean logic may be applied in both card-based and computer-based information-retrieval systems. Boolean logic is important in computerized index systems. It is used to support the framing of search profiles for use both in retrospective searching of databases and in producing current-awareness services, particularly SDI (selective dissemination of information). In such applications the search statement, usually referred to as a user interest profile, is a linked set of index terms which remains relatively stable over several computer runs. The search statement is matched against the indexing assigned to the latest batch of document records that have been input to the system. The terms linked by the search logic may be drawn from free or controlled indexing languages. Profiles will usually need to be more complex with free-language searching as greater provision for the entry of documents under synonyms and related terms is necessary. The search profile is fixed for the duration of any given search, and will be modified only periodically as the quality of the set of notifications output from the search drops to unacceptable levels.

Fig. 8.1 An example of an online search

```
HELLO FROM SDC/ORBIT IV. (03/14/85   8:57 A.M.   PACIFIC TIME
ENTER SECURITY CODE:
+ + 0000000000                                                    ①
YOU ARE NOW CONNECTED TO THE METALS DATAFILE DATABASE.
COPYRIGHT 1982 METALS INFORMATION
COVERS THROUGH NOV (8411)

*PROXIMITY – SEARCHABLE*

DISCLAIMER: NUMERICAL VALUES CONTAINED IN THIS DATABASE ARE       ②
REPORTED FROM
WIDE-RANGING SOURCES. DO NOT USE THESE DATA VALUES FOR DESIGN
PURPOSES WITHOUT CONFIRMATION THROUGH THE DATA SOURCE GIVEN.

SS 1 /C?
USER:                                                             ③
INCONEL617/DS,SP

PROG:
SS 1 PSTG (16)

SS 2 /C?
USER:                                                             ④
1 AND B/FS

PROG:
            OCCURS      TERM
             17258      B/FS
SS 2 PSTG (8)

SS 3 /C?
USER:
PRT FU 1-1

PROG:

–1–
AN    – 840508076
XR    84 – 311912
FS    B
TI    – Effect of Vacuum Environment on High Temperature Low Cycle
         Fatigue Properties of Inconel 617.
SO    – J. Soc. Mater. Sci., Jpn., June 1983, 32, (357), 667
DT    – Measured
LO    – Japan
AC    – NI (NICKEL BASE-ALLOYS); SP (SUPERALLOYS)
NO    – SN diagrams given
CO    – C 0.09; Si 0.14; Mn 0.02, S 0.002; Cr 21.9; Co 12.4; Mo 8.96; Al 1.28;
         Ti 0.57; Fe 0.44; base Ni (WT%)
MF    – C.Al.Co.Cr.Fe.Mn.Mo.Ni.S.Si.Ti
DS    – Inconel617
PROP  –TEMPERATURE; TM = Room (T20T040)                           ⑤
         CONDITION; CO = Hardened (1177 deg C, 1 hr, water quenched)
            TENSILE STRENGTH; TN = 765 MPa
            0.2% PROOF TENSILE STRENGTH; PT = 330 MPa
            ELONGATION; EL = 56 %
            REDUCTION/AA; RA = 46 %
PROP  –TEMPERATURE; TM = 900 deg C (T800T0900; T900T01000)
         CONDITION; CO = Hardened (1177 deg, 1 hr, water quenched)
            TENSILE STRENGTH; TN = 216 MPa
            0.2% PROOF TENSILE RENGTx; PT = 128 Pa
            ELONGATION; EL = 68 %
            REDUCTION/AREA; RA = 62 %
PROP  –TEMPERATURE; TM = 1000 deg C ( 900T01000; TI000T0120 ) ;
         TI000T020 ⟨0)
         CONDITION; CO = Hardened (1177 deg C, 1 hr, water quenched)
            TENSILE STRENGTH; TN = 132 MPa
            0.2% PROOF TENSILE STRENGTH; PT = 74 MPa
            ELONGATION; EL = 78 %
            REDUCTION/AREA; RA = 66 %

SS 3 /C?
USER:
LOGOFF Y

PROG:
TERMINAL SESSION FINISHED 03/14/85   9:00 A.M. (PACIFIC TIME)
ELAPSED TIME ON MDF/1: 0.06 HRS.                                  ⑥
ELAPSED TIME THIS TERMINAL SESSION: 0.06 HOURS.
PLEASE HANG UP YOUR TELEPHONE NOW. GOOD-BYE!

CLR PAD  (00)   00:00:047 55 14
```

A designer requires information about the corrosion resistance and other properties of a nickel-based superalloy, INCONEL 617.

1. The searcher connects his terminal to the SDC (System Development Corporation) host computer system on which Metals Datafile is available. A unique password will enable you to do this.

2. The disclaimer as to the contents of Metals Datafile appears.

3. The search strategy is entered. Note that, with Metals Datafile, you can search for alloys by name. Since we know INCONEL 617 is either a description or a specification, the search can be limited to the alloy designation (DS) or alloy specification (SP) fields.

4 The host computer tells us that Metals Datafile contains a total of 16 records relating to INCONEL 617. As the enquiry relates to numerical data only, the search is further limited to the numerical subfile (segment B).

The host computer informs us that 'Subfile B' contains a total of 17,258 records, of which just 8 relate to this particular alloy.

5. The first of the eight records is displayed online. If the record shown is relevant to the searcher's needs, the records can either be printed to your own printer, they can be printed offline and mailed to you.

If the data is contained in an article, the Metals Information Document Delivery Service can deliver a copy of the original article to you within 24 hours of your request.

If, as is the case here, the original article is in a foreign language, our Translations Service can supply an English version on request. The record shown here comes from an article in the Journal of the Japanese Society of Materials Science.

6. The host computer is instructed to terminate the session. The time taken is displayed, and the computer disconnects. For a search of 0.1 of an hour with 8 online prints, the cost would be approximately £10/$15 including communications cost.

Think how long it would take you to locate this information without Metals Datafile!

Fig. 8.2 Boolean logic operators

Operator	Search type	Venn diagrams	Meaning
AND	Conjunctive		Logical product, symbolized by A AND B, A, B, A × B or (A)(B). Both index terms A and B must be assigned to a document for a match, eg Health × Safety × Oil × Industry implies that all of the above four terms must have been assigned to a document for a match.
OR	Additive		Logical sum, symbolized by A OR B, or A + B. Only one of the two index terms A or B need be associated with a document for a match. This operator is usually introduced when A and B can be regarded as equivalent for the purposes of the search, eg Coal OR Coke would serve to retrieve all documents with either the term Coal or the term Coke assigned.
NOT	Subtractive		Logical difference, symbolized by A NOT B, or A−B. The index term must be assigned, and assigned in the absence of the term B for a match, eg Computer × Storage × Medium−Magnetic Tape requires all documents on computer storage media except those on magnetic tape.

The notifications may be printed or made available for viewing on a screen via a computer network.

The profiles constructed and developed during the process of a retrospective online search are fundamentally similar to those profiles suitable for current-awareness services. The essential distinction lies in the fact that online search profiles are constructed and modified, at least to some extent, during the actual search. Search strategies may be amended to take account of knowledge gained about a subject and its literature as the search progresses. Another feature distinguishes retrospective and current-awareness searches. Although this is inevitably a generalization, it is normally the case that profiles for retrospective searching specify a much more restricted subject area, and hence may involve more complex logical statements than equivalent current-awareness profiles. A user expects a current-awareness service to keep him abreast of developments in most, if not all, of his interests. A retrospective search is usually conducted in respect of a specific problem or task. Nevertheless, the logical devices that are available for current-awareness searching and retrospective retrieval are often the same.

In an online retrospective search, the profile is evolved or modified as the search progresses. The statements are framed one at a time, and feedback is available at each stage, hence the term interactive searching. For instance, a request posed to the computer to search for the occurrence of an individual term usually results in a statement which gives the number of documents whose records are stored in association with that term, such as

1   746   SHRUBS

At any stage in the search the result of linking terms by the search logic of the system can be viewed. A request to the computer such as

COMBINE 1 AND 3

where 1 and 3 are sets of documents that have previously been noted, leads to something of the form:

4   6   COMBINE 1 AND 3

Here the number of documents satisfying the previous logic statement (i.e. 6 documents) is indicated. With this type of facility search strategy can be refined to give the most profitable output. Further complex search strategies are possible with the intercession of other kinds of logic (see below) and the use of brackets. The example search in figure 8.3 shows how the statements in an online search make use of Boolean logic operators.

Boolean logic operators can be represented in a Peek-a-boo or optical coincidence card index with term records by the combination of cards

Fig. 8.3 An example search showing the evolution of a search strategy

Search input	Search output		Comments
SELECT PRESTEL	1	40	Searches for all records with PRESTEL as a term. Set number 1 comprises those records with PRESTEL as a term and includes 40 records
SELECT GATES-HEAD	2	50	Searches for all records with GATESHEAD as a term. Set number 2 comprises those records with JOURNAL as a term and includes 50 records
COMBINE 1 AND 2	3	4	Searches for all records with both PRESTEL AND GATESHEAD as terms. Set number 3 comprises those records with both PRESTEL and GATESHEAD as terms and includes 4 records
TYPE 3/6/1	AN EXPERI-MENT INTO TELE-SHOPPING IN GATESHEAD USING PRESTEL		Displays the first item in set 3 in format 6 (titles only). Title displayed.
SELECT TELE-SHOPPING	4	10	Search for all records with TELESHOPPING as a term. Set number 4 comprises those records with TELE-SHOPPING as a term and includes 10 records

in various ways. Boolean logic operators may also be used in searches of item-entry edge notch card systems.

Weighted-term search logic
In most search statements or document profiles it is possible to designate

certain concepts as being more significant than their neighbours. Weights are a quantitative measure of the prominence of various index terms in the description of a subject. This section discusses the use of weights in search profiles, but it should be noted that it is also possible to assign weights to the concepts in document profiles, i.e. to indicate the primary concepts in a document and discriminate between these and subsidiary concepts.

In its role in formulating search profiles, weighted-term logic may be introduced either as a search logic in its own right, or as a means of reducing the search output from a search whose basic logic is Boolean.

In an application where weighted-term logic is the primary search logic, search profiles are framed by combining index terms in a simple logical sum. Each term is assigned a weight which reflects its significance in determining the relevance of a document to the search question, and document references worthy of printing are selected on the basis of a threshold weight. A simple SDI profile using weighted-term search logic is displayed below:

Search description – the language and social behaviour of educationally subnormal children

Search profile

8 Language
7 Communication
6 Behaviour
5 Interaction
4 Subnormal
3 E S N
2 Handicapped
1 Children

A threshold weight appropriate to the specificity of the searcher's enquiry must be established. For instance, a threshold weight of 15 would retrieve all documents with the following combinations of terms assigned:

Language and Communication
Communication, Behaviour and Interaction
Subnormal, ESN and Language
Handicapped, Subnormal, Children and Language

But documents with the following terms assigned would be rejected on the grounds that their combined weights did not exceed the pre-selected threshold:

Children and Handicapped
ESN, Handicapped and Children
Interaction and Children

A different threshold weight would cause either a larger or smaller set of documents to be selected as being relevant. By modifying the threshold weight the search specifications can be broadened or narrowed.

Weighted-term search logic may also be used to supplement Boolean logic. Here, weighted-term logic is a means of limiting or ranking the output from a search that has been conducted in response to a search profile framed using Boolean logic. In the process of the search, prior to display or printing, the computer ranks references according to their weighting, and only those documents with sufficiently high rankings will be deemed relevant and eventually retrieved. This combination of search logics is most likely to be effective where a relatively complex search statement is required to be satisfied, and where documents may be deemed relevant with different combinations of assigned terms present. Documents that satisfy the logical statement are first sought, and from this first set are selected those documents with total weights that exceed the threshold weight. The example below demonstrates, with a relatively straightforward search topic, how weighted-term search logic can be used to refine the output from a search, and to reject those documents that are likely to be of only peripheral interest:

Search description—the opportunities for further and higher education for the disabled student

Search profile

A	Further	5
B	Higher	5
C	University	4
D	Polytechnic	4
E	College	3
F	Disabled	5
G	Handicapped	5
H	Students	1

(A OR B OR C OR D OR E) AND (F OR G) AND (H)

The weights in the right-hand column will determine whether or not the document is retrieved in response to a search. Again it is possible to select threshold weights in such a way that less relevant documents are not retrieved.

Other retrieval facilities

There are a number of other search facilities that are common in computer-based information-retrieval systems. Many of these facilities are particularly appropriate when searching the full text of a database or in other circumstances where the search terms are not drawn from a controlled indexing language, but they are also useful when searching on controlled indexing language terms.

1 *Search refinement* A basic feature of all post-coordinate indexing systems is that it should be possible to search for a set of records meeting certain criteria, and then from that set to select a further set of those that also match an additional criterion, thus either broadening or

narrowing the original search and either expanding or reducing the original set. This can be achieved in various ways. One of the most flexible is to give each record set selected a set number so that the set number can be used in framing search statements, maybe several stages later in the search. Figure 8.4 demonstrates this process.

Fig. 8.4 An example of a current-awareness search on PsycAlert

TOPIC: Research on employee assistance programs for alcoholism or drug abuse. This search was executed on DIALOG.

?s (addiction or alcoholism)/de or drug dependency or drug abuse or problem drinking } User requests the system to search for a series of terms

```
     2539  ADDICTION/DE
     6001  ALCOHOLISM/DE
      858  DRUG DEPENDENCY
     2027  DRUG ABUSE
      374  PROBLEM DRINKING
SI  10788  (ADDICTION OR ALCOHOL-
            ISM)/DE OR DRUG DEPEND-
            ENCY OR DRUG ABUSE OR
            PROBLEM DRINKING
```
} System responds with numbers of documents including those terms

?s employee?(f)program?/ti,id,de — User conducts a further search

```
     5380  EMPLOYEE?/TI,ID,DE
    27853  PROGRAM?/TI,ID,DE
S2    307  EMPLOYEE?/(F)PROGRAM?/
            TI,ID,DE
```
} System responds again

?s s1 and s2 — User requests that documents in both sets s1 and s2 be identified

```
   10788  S1
     307  S2
S3    22  S1 AND S2
```
} System identifies 22 records of potential relevance to the search

SAMPLE RECORD:

73-10637
   Management styles, perceptions of substance abuse, and employee assistance programs in organizations.
      Steele, Paul D.; Hubbard, Robert L.
      U New Mexico, Albuquerque
      Journal of Applied Behavioral Science, 1985 Vol 21(3) 271-286
ISSN: 00218863
      Journal Announcement: 7304
      Language: ENGLISH   Document Type: JOURNAL ARTICLE
      Examined the relationships among organizational style, perceptions of the extent of substance abuse, and the structure and processes of employee assistance programs (EAPs) in the work place to identify factors associated with the extent of substance abuse and the provision of effective services to abusers within organizations. The Survey of Organizations (SOO)

119

Fig. 8.4 continued

and additional questions relating to substance use were administered to a random sample of 760 employees from 7 corporations, and in-depth, open-ended interviews were conducted with 83 EAP staff and corporate administrators. Results show the following: (1) There was a negative correlation between organizational climate and satisfaction (as measured by the SOO indices) and the extent of substance abuse in the work place; (2) the majority of Ss were unaware of specific organizational and EAP policies and procedures; and (3) EAPs tended to be poorly integrated in terms of structure and process with the organizations' administrative hierarchy. Targets for information campaigns and means of integrating EAPs into the corporate hierarchy are suggested. (42 ref)

Descriptors: MANAGEMENT METHODS (29380); DRUG ABUSE (15220); EMPLOYEE ASSISTANCE PROGRAMS (17015); PERSONNEL (37980); ORGANIZATIONAL CLIMATE (35710); ADULTHOOD (01150)

Identifiers: management style & perceptions of extent of substance abuse & characteristics of employee assistance programs within organizations, employees & program staff & corporate administrators

Section Headings: 3650 (ORGANIZATIONAL BEHAVIOR & JOB SATISFACTION)

---

2 *Truncation and text-string searching* Truncation and the ability to search on word strings or character strings are available in almost all computerized post-coordinate indexing environments. Searching with truncated stems enables the searcher to search simultaneously for a number of words with the same stem. For example, NATION£ might cause the records with this stem included to be retrieved, such as those including NATIONALITY, NATIONALITIES, NATIONALIZATION, NATIONALIZE, NATIONALISM, NATIONAL. The ability to search on word stems is particularly valuable where the text to be searched is in free-language format, and where there is a need to compound synonyms, such as where words with common stems and similar meanings have been entered. In this respect, truncation achieves the same result as linking word variants with OR, without the searcher needing to specify all of the variants. Clearly, this removes the onus from the searcher to list all of the variants. Truncation can be achieved by right-hand truncation, left-hand truncation, or masking of letters in the middle of a word. Right-hand truncation involves specifying the stem to begin a word, e.g. NATION£. Left-hand truncation involves specifying the stem to finish a word, e.g. £CHLORIDE. Both right- and left-hand truncation may be employed simulataneously, e.g. £CHLOR£. The masking of letters in the middle of a word is particularly useful for language variants, e.g. NA£IONAL will cause a search for records with NATIONAL and

NACIONAL. Sometimes referred to as a wildcard, masking in the middle of the word can involve constraints on the number of characters included, but on other occasions, any number of characters can be acceptable for a match. For example, in Henco's INFO, SPA \ will search for SPA with any number of characters following: including, for example, SPAIN, SPANISH, SPAGHETTI, etc. and also SPA. However, SPA % \ excludes SPA itself by including a wildcard character and specifying that the string must be at least four characters long. This is clearly useful for searching for a particular name when the exact spelling is unknown.

Searching on right-hand truncated word stems is easy for the computer to perform, since the alphabetical ordering of the index will ensure that all words with the same lexical stem will be stored in adjacent locations. However, string searching of the kind required for letters in the middle of words is time-consuming in an alphabetically ordered index, and normally this type of searching is restricted to small, well-defined sections of the database. For example, in INFO, RES 'CIVIL WAR' will search for words represented by the string of characters CIVIL WAR.

3 *Contextual logic* Contextual logic operators make it possible to specify the location of terms with respect to one another. For example, the BRS/SEARCH positional operators are shown in figure 8.5. To take a further example, in CONCORD from Bytesmiths Ltd the abbreviation SEEDS W/20 TECHNOLOGY specifies that the two words must be found within 20 words of one another. The command W/ requires that the first word be immediately adjacent to the second. For example, SHELTERED W/HOUSING will search for the phrase SHELTERED HOUSING.

Fig. 8.5 BRS/SEARCH positional operators

Operator	Example	Result
SAME	library *same* microcomputers	Finds any document in which 'library' and 'microcomputers' appear in the *same paragraph* of the document.
WITH	library *with* microcomputers	Finds any document in which 'library' and 'microcomputers' appear in the *same sentence* of the document.
NEAR	library *near 10* micro-computers	Finds any document in which 'library' and 'microcomputers' appear *within 10 words of each other* (either may occur first).
ADJ	library *adj* microcomputers	Finds any document in which 'library' is *adjacent to* 'micro-computers'.

4 *Field searching* The ability to search for the occurrence of terms in specific fields within the record makes it possible to be more precise in searching. For example, in BRS/SEARCH, MAKEPEACE.AU. finds any document where MAKEPEACE appears in the author (AU) paragraph. In STATUS, 'standards @ abstract?' retrieves all those articles in which the word 'standards' appears in the 'abstract' section. In TRIP, FIND SNAME=PETER JONES locates PETER JONES in a name field.

5 *Range searching* Other operators permit the selection of documents meeting certain criteria. Thus, in STAIRS the following operators may be used in conjunction with the ..SELECT command:

EQ meaning 'equal to'   LT meaning 'less than'
NE meaning 'not equal to'   NL meaning 'not less than'
GT meaning 'greater than'   WL meaning 'within the limits'
NG meaning 'not greater than'   OL meaning 'outside the limits'

For example, 2 DATE NL 870716 will cause the listing of documents with entries in the date field of dates after 16 July 1987, whilst 3 DATE OL 860101,870101 will cause the listing of all documents with dates not in 1986.

6 *Command languages* Most text-retrieval systems offer a user interface based on commands, rather than a menu-based approach, although menu-based systems are also available.

A command language is the set of commands or instructions that the searcher uses to instruct the computer to perform certain operations. Negus[1] has identified 14 basic functions for which commands must be present in any information-retrieval command language. This set of commands forms the basis for the Euronet Common Command Language. These same functions are also seen to be important in framing the International Standard for Command Languages. These command functions are:

CONNECT   to provide for logging on
BASE   to identify the database to be searched
FIND   to input a search term
DISPLAY   to display a list of alphabetically linked terms
RELATE   to display logically related terms
SHOW   to print references online
PRINT   to print references offline
FORMAT   to specify the format to be displayed
DELETE   to delete search terms or print requests

[1] Negus, A.E., 'Development of the Euronet Diane Common Command Language', in *Proceedings of the 3rd International Online Information Meeting, London, 4-6 December 1979*, Oxford, Learned Information, 1979, pp.95-8.

SAVE	to save a search formulation for later use on the same or another database on the same system
OWN	to use a system's own command when the general system, in this case Euronet, does not cater for a specialized function available on a particular system
STOP	to end the session and log off
MORE	to request the system to display more information, for instance, to continue the alphabetical display of terms
HELP	to obtain guidance online when in difficulty

It is possible to search some of the larger hosts using the Common Command Language. Some packages for in-house use, such as MIMER (from Savant Enterprises), offer an interface based on the Common Command Language. However, in general, the different systems and hosts use different command languages, depending on the retrieval software. Users would prefer standardization of command languages, since the need to become familiar with different command languages is a barrier to effective retrieval.

8.5 Conclusion

These search and retrieval facilities have been discussed in this chapter on post-coordinate indexing because they are virtually essential for searching in any system where the index terms, be they controlled or natural language, represent single concepts. Any coordination of concepts must take place at the search stage because it is not present in the original record. This statement is restricted to coordination of concepts as the indexer would recognize it. Of course, the text of documents or titles is full of coordinated concepts but, as a searcher, it is difficult to exploit these concept coordinations fully because of the unpredictable nature of their representation. For example, precisely which preposition, conjunction or verb, may link two coordinated concepts? So, in practice, instead of exploiting the rich coordination of natural language, most systems ignore these links between concepts and resort to picking words from text at random and using Boolean logic operators and other devices to coordinate concepts in a search profile. These coordinated concepts in the search profile may or may not match coordinated concepts in the record and, thus, by neglecting the concept coordination that is present in natural language, we introduce the possibility of *false drops* or *noise*. Our search profile, for example, might specify History AND Science where it is intended to represent our statement for a search on the history of science. With this we will retrieve any records indexed under the word History and under the word Science. This may include documents on, for example:

the history of science
the science of history

the science and history of genetics
the effects of science on history
the effects of history on science
to offer only a few of the more likely examples.

The problems surrounding the neglect of concept coordination as it is to be found in the document were recognized in the early days of card-based post-coordinate indexes. Two devices, roles and links, were introduced to store coordination between terms in the original document. Roles were codes assigned to concepts to represent the role that a specific concept played in a given document. Links were also codes, but they were used to link two coordinated concepts in the index, so that this coordination could be taken into account during searching. Neither of these two devices have been extensively exploited in computer-based information-retrieval systems. False drops are perhaps less of an annoyance in a computer-based system when brief records can be quickly scanned and rejected as necessary, but it would still be more satisfactory if they did not arise!

Having proclaimed the merits of pre-coordination in effective and efficient retrieval, the next chapter examines pre-coordinate indexing systems in greater detail. Most of the systems mentioned in Chapter 9 are concerned with the applications of pre-coordinate indexing in printed indexes. Although this is an important area of application of pre-coordinate indexing systems, pre-coordinated index strings are used as search terms in computer-based information-retrieval systems and can be searched using all of the devices outlined in the last section. A more detailed discussion of this point is given in the section on PRECIS indexing in Chapter 9.

Chapter 9

PRE-COORDINATE INDEXING SYSTEMS

9.1 Principles

Post-coordinate indexing is one approach to the problem of providing adequate access to complex subjects which are comprised of a number of single concepts all of which may be valid access points. Pre-coordinate indexing is another line of attack. Like post-coordinate indexing, pre-coordinate indexing procedures are preoccupied primarily with the index entries that must be generated in order that complex subjects can be satisfactorily retrieved. But, unlike post-coordinate indexes, the subjects represented in pre-coordinate indexes are shown with all of the component concepts coordinated. Such coordination or linking of concepts that is present in the subjects as they are to be entered in the index is recognized at the indexing stage and retained in any index entries subsequently generated. Thus, the entries in an index based upon pre-coordination are as complex as is necessary to describe the subject.

The nature of the subjects to be tackled by pre- and post-coordinate indexing is common. Complex or composite subjects demand a series of entries and terms in order that they be described adequately. Two examples of such subjects are:

- Noise from pumps used in association with microbore central heating in houses
- Computerized control systems for nuclear reactors

These two subjects may be described respectively by the following strings of index terms:

- Noise, Pumps, Microbore heating, Housing
- Computers, Control systems, Nuclear reactors.

Plainly, any of the terms listed for each of the topics would represent a valid approach in attempting to retrieve documents on the given topic. Pre-coordinate indexing generates indexes which contain headings which incorporate all of the individual concepts, in contrast to post-coordinate indexing where index headings cover only one single concept. Thus, for the two examples introduced above, in a pre-coordinate index the following might be satisfactory and typical index headings:

125

- Housing: Heating, Microbore: Pumps: Noise
- Nuclear reactors: Control systems: Computers.

The individual concepts recorded in such headings may be akin to those evident in post-coordinate indexes, and may even be described by the same terms. However, the manner in which they contribute to the formulation of an index differs.

Pre-coordination eliminates the need for sophisticated search logic. The index user merely looks under the terms that he expects to find the subject described with, and, with a good index, finds and follows instructions from his first entry point until sufficient and appropriate document references have been retrieved. Pre-coordinate indexes require no special features in their physical format. Many indexes that reflect pre-coordinate indexing principles are hard-copy printed indexes. Some of these indexes are totally independent of the computer, but others exploit the capacity of the computer in formatting and display of entries. Pre-coordinate indexing principles are evident to a limited extent in online or batch-searched computer-based information-retrieval systems, as will be discussed further later in this chapter. Printed indexes that incorporate to varying degrees the principles of pre-coordinate indexing are to be found in abstracting and indexing journals, national bibliographies, and indexes to journals, to name but a few examples. Pre-coordinate indexing principles have also found some application in subject indexes to library catalogues and the shelf arrangement of book stock. The type of environment in which the principles of pre-coordination are workable are restricted by the acceptable bulk or length of index headings. Very specific or exhaustive indexing would create index headings with more components than is desirable. Headings exceeding a given length, the length depending upon the application, are unpredictable and difficult to remember and handle. Also, the number of references or entries required to index one document, if exhaustive indexing is attempted, would lead to a very bulky index.

Two issues recur in all pre-coordinate indexes. The first issue concerns the consistent description of subjects. With many-concept headings consistency must be instilled both into the terms used to describe the individual concepts that comprise the multiple-concept heading and also into the order in which those individual concept terms are cited or listed. Before a consistent citation order can be achieved, some principles must be established and agreed concerning the acceptable citation order. At the two extremes, the order may simply be decided for each topic as and when it arises, and followed thereafter, or some theoretical basis or rules for the ordering of terms or concepts may be derived. A theoretical basis to citation order should produce a more highly structured system whose objective is to achieve consistent citation orders between similar, yet distinct, subjects. The description of one subject by two different headings with different terms and citation orders is less likely to be overlooked if some rationale determines the order that should be adopted. However, many indexing systems have evolved over the last century, and have their roots in a time when detailed specification of subjects was unnecessary. Indexes based on traditional subject headings lists tend to use very little structuring of citation order; citation orders need not be comparable between subjects, nor is there any comprehensive set of principles that determines the citation order that is selected. Yet even these indexes recognize some rules concerning the structure of headings. Examples both of traditional less formalized pre-coordinate indexing systems and also of indexes with more highly structured approaches to citation order, will be considered in the next section.

The second issue that all indexers must consider is the need to provide access for those users who approach the subject under consideration for indexing from one of the 'secondary' concepts. Only one term can appear in the primary position in the prescribed citation order. The preferred citation order should be that order which is believed to match the approach of many of the users who can be expected to retrieve information on the topic. No citation order, no matter how well founded, will prove suitable for every searcher. References or added entries must supplement the first or main entry and cater for access from other angles. At least one reference or added entry is usually deemed to be necessary from each of the 'secondary' concepts in the preferred order. In the same way that citation orders may have more or less theoretical foundations, equally, reference generation may follow a predetermined pattern, or the reference or added entries to be included may be designed on an ad hoc basis. Usually there is some pattern to the generation of additional references in order to keep the number of auxiliary references to an acceptable level. Also, if a simple algorithm for the generation of index entries can be stated, then additional entries and references can be printed by computer, using the primary index string as input data. Various methods of reference generation will be reviewed in a later section.

Both of the above issues arise because pre-coordinate systems are fundamentally one-place systems. One-place systems are convenient under circumstances where it is desirable to have only one main entry for each document, as in many bibliographies and catalogues. Such systems may also have advantages for the searcher. A number of searches can be conducted simultaneously, by tracing entries under similar headings. Also, search strategy can be modified relatively easily, where only refinements or slight modifications in index terms are appropriate.

Citation order
We have already noted the effect of citation order on the operation of

an index based on alphabetical subject headings. Very early in the history of alphabetical subject headings it was recognized that headings should be formulated in accordance with some principles. The search for appropriate principles has occupied indexers for most of this century. The forerunner of many more recent ideas was Charles Ammi Cutter.

Cutter's rules for a dictionary catalogue
These were published in 1876, and form one of the earlier codifications of the problems and some solutions concerning the alphabetical subject approach. The issue of citation orders for composite subjects is not considered systematically and Cutter's recommendations serve more to illustrate problems than to demonstrate solutions. Cutter selected headings on the basis that headings in a catalogue should be those terms that are in general usage, and are accepted by educated people. In addition to problems with new subjects which lacked 'accepted' or established names, this guiding principle engendered inconsistency in the form of headings. Equally, Cutter's devotion to natural language posed problems with multi-word terms. Sometimes the natural-language ordering of words in a term would cause filing of the term under the first and possibly less significant term. To avoid unhelpful sequences, Cutter argued that when it could be established that the second term was definitely more significant then inversion of headings was acceptable. This was all very tidy, but who was to judge significance?

Despite the inconsistencies inherent in Cutter's fundamental premises, he did give some guidance on citation order under certain specialized conditions. For example, he believed that where subject and place are both elements of a topic, subject should precede place in scientific and related areas, but that place should take precedence in areas such as history, government and commerce. For the humanities, e.g. literature and art, the adjectival form of the country or language is recommended, e.g. German poetry.

Cutter's practices and policies were a starting point and remain important today because they are embodied in the Library of Congress List of Subject Headings and Sears' List of Subject Headings. Both of these lists are widely used in dictionary catalogues in the United States. These lists have evolved through several editions with no radical modification to meet modern problems. Composite subjects were less prevalent in Cutter's day and principles in subject-heading formulation were less vital. The information that most modern indexes must organize emerges in greater quantities and concerns much more complex subjects than Cutter could have anticipated. The sheer bulk of the headings and the complexity of reference structures in a dictionary catalogue based on the Library of Congress Subject Headings is sufficient to confirm that a more systematic approach might prove fruitful.

Kaiser's systematic indexing

This embodies the first consistent approach to the problems of significance order. The treatise arose from Kaiser's work in indexing information relating to business and industry. Kaiser's stepping-off point was the observation that many composite subjects can be analysed into a combination of a concrete and a process. He suggested that if subjects with these two components were cited in the order first Concrete, then Process, that the headings thus produced would usually coincide with natural-language usage to some extent. Thus a document on the 'Servicing of ships' may be indexed under 'Ships: Servicing'. Where place is one of the concepts present in a subject Kaiser makes a double entry, once under the concrete and once under place. Thus a document on 'Shipbuilding in Japan' would be entered under each of the two headings: 'Shipbuilding—Japan' and 'Japan—Shipbuilding'. One problem on which Kaiser alighted was that many processes can be further analysed into a concrete and a process; for example, 'Steelmaking' can become 'Steel: Production'. This feature hinders consistency because some subjects have potential for being analysed in different ways. Kaiser also investigated the effect of grouping subheadings of a subject. Rather than straight alphabetical arrangement subheadings are grouped according to their subject. For example, all subheadings representing processes may be grouped and precede those referring to places. This may help in subject organization, but one of the main advantages of an alphabetical sequence, its self-evident order, is sacrificed in the process.

Coates and British technology index (now Current technology index)

E J Coates made one of the most significant contributions to the formulation of subject headings. His ideas are embodied in *British technology index* (now *Current technology index*), of which he was the editor for many years. Coates started his study of citation order by noting Kaiser's theories of Concrete-Process and reaffirmed this aspect of Kaiser's work. Coates went on to evolve rules to cater for the citation orders appropriate to a wide range of composite subjects. Kaiser's Concrete-Process was re-labelled Thing-Action. Coates believed that in order to conceptualize an action it is necessary to visualize the thing on which the action is being performed. This principle was used to establish an extended citation order:

Thing—Part—Material—Action

According to Coates this results in headings whose first component is the most likely to come into the mind of the searcher. The following headings show the citation order advanced by Coates:

- Steel, low alloy: Welding, electron beam
- Steel: Production: Coking: Coal: Blending: Plant
- Sugar cane: Harvester
- Technical colleges: Piles; Concrete, bored: Testing: Ultrasonics
- Television: Transmission: Computers.

Note that the headings when read backwards with appropriate prepositions inserted make a title-like phrase describing the subject. Thus, often index headings derive easily from natural-language order by straight inversion and the omission of prepositions. Figure 9.1 provides an extract from *Current technology index*.

Fig. 9.1 An extract from Current technology index

RADIO : Receivers
See
Motor cars : Radio receivers
RADIO : Telephony
See
Telephony : Radio

RADIO, V.H.F.

50MHz: long-awaited band available 1 February.
Radio Communication, 62 (Jan 86) p.18-23
Receivers : Modifications
Converting the 'Colt 295' 40/80-channel
a.m./f.m. c.b. set for use on the 10-metre
amateur band, pt.2. R. Alban, *Short Wave
Magazine*, 43 (Jan 86) p.458-60

RADIOACTIVATION ANALYSIS
Related headings
Neutron activation analysis

RADIOACTIVE MATERIALS

Waste : Disposal : Great Britain
Management and disposal of radioactive waste.
[Nuclear Industry Radioactive Waste Executive
(NIREX)] M.E. Ginniff & I.M. Blair, *Energy
World*, (Jan 86) p.5-7

RADIOGRAPHY
See
Steel, Mild, Welded, Butt : Radiography
RADIOISOTOPES
See
Air—Water : Interfaces : Mass transfer : Studies :
Radioisotopes

Chain indexing
This is chiefly a technique for constructing an organized set of entries for the subject index to a classified catalogue. This index both provides access to the classified sequence by indicating where subjects may be found, and also records some connections between topics that are not evident from the classified sequence. The index entries are created according to a pattern which is derived from the hierarchical structure underlying the classification scheme. The intention is to create the minimum set of entries necessary for effective access. The discussion is best demonstrated by examining the hierarchy and index entries of one subject. Suppose it is desired to index 'Victorian period English poetry'. The classification number for this topic in the Dewey Decimal Classification Scheme is 821.8 and the hierarchy in this area of the schedule may be analysed thus:

Hierarchy (or chain)
    8   Literature
        2   English
            1   Poetry
                .8   Victorian period
Index entries (according to chain indexing)
Victorian period: Poetry: English: Literature   821.8
Poetry: English: Literature   821
English: Literature   820
Literature   800

These index entries show clearly the way in which index entries are constructed. Individual concepts in the chain are treated in accordance with a rigid citation order. But this order has no theoretical basis distinct from the basis on which the scheme is ordered; the citation order is a function of the classification scheme. A more thorough account of the concept of citation order in relation to classification schemes is to be found in other texts, such as Buchanan, B., *Theory of library classification*, Bingley, 1979.

Articulated subject indexes
These are based on title-like phrases that have some conventions concerning citation order, but these conventions do not require any theoretical structure which recognizes concept categories. The title-like phrase combines concepts in the order in which they would be listed in a sentence or phrase. For example, an indexing string for an articulated subject index might take the form:

<Soil-resistant <Finishing> of <Carpets> and <Wall-coverings>

where the brackets are used to designate terms that are to appear as index headings. The indexer then expresses the subject using a stylized English sentence and the computer generates a series of entries with a complete subject statement at every entry point. The computer is programmed to recognize cues such as prepositions and punctuation, and thus generates a series of entries each comprising an entry term and a qualifying phrase.

9.3 Reference structure

In order to permit the index user to approach a composite heading via one of the concepts that does not take the first position in the citation order it is necessary to consider how access may be provided to secondary concepts. Remember that it is also possible that a user will approach the index with a synonym or related term to one of those used to describe concepts in the headings. Links between related terms and synonymous terms must also be a feature of the index. But for now we will concentrate on access to the secondary concepts in the primary citation order. Each type of pre-coordinate indexing system must incorporate some rules for the generation of references or added entries. Many systems rely upon moving the index terms in the heading through the various positions in the heading. Particularly if the computer is to be responsible for creating a series of headings from one index string, it is desirable that there be some algorithm for the generation of references and added entries. Also, economy dictates that not every possible entry can be printed. Consider a complex heading with six individual concepts. Obviously, for each term to appear in the lead position at least six entries are necessary. If it is intended that each term occupy each position in a heading, the largest number of possible distinct headings or arrangements of the index terms is 720. Obviously this is far too many references or added entries. Some means must be found of selecting from the 720 possible entries those which are the most helpful. Several different solutions to this problem have been tried. Cutter recommended a network of references and recognized that a systematic approach to reference structure was necessary in order to produce an effective index. However, in the interests of economy, he restricted links to downward references leading from broader to narrower subjects, and largely ignored upwards and sideways links. This practice is continued in dictionary catalogues but is of limited success and makes little contribution to the structure of references that is necessary to cater for a composite subject.

Chain indexing creates a number of index entries, as shown in the previous example. The second and subsequent entries cater for the hidden terms in the first entry. Each heading becomes at the same time simpler and less specific. *Current technology index* also bases its reference structure on chain procedure. The first reference comprises all of the components in the heading, but in inverted order. The second reference retains the order of the first (i.e. inverted), but the first element of the preferred citation order is removed. Other references follow, with the progressive removal of terms. If A, B, C and D are index terms chain procedure creates the following four entries:

A B C D
B C D
C D
D

or the following entries for a document on 'the inspection of the painting of steel structures':

Inspection : Painting : Steel : Structures
Painting : Steel : Structures
Steel : Structures
Structures.

The reference structure used in PRECIS indexing will be more fully developed later. Known as shunting, the following entries would be created with A, B, C and D as index terms.

1 A
      B C D
2 B A
      C D
3 C B A
      D
4 D C B A

which with the example above would lead to entries such as:

1 Structures
      Steel Painting Inspection
2 Steel structures
      Painting Inspection
3 Painting Steel structures
      Inspection
4 Inspection Painting Steel structures

Other approaches to the movement of the components of index headings in order to generate additional entries are also possible. Three techniques are cycled or cyclic indexing, rotated indexing and SLIC indexing. Cycled indexing involves the movement of the lead term to the last position in the subsequent entry. This process is repeated until each concept has occupied the lead position. Rotated indexing involves each element in turn becoming the heading under which an entry is filed, but no change in citation order takes place. SLIC indexing, or Selective Listing in Combination, involves the combination of elements, but in one direction only. These techniques are demonstrated below:

133

Cyclic indexing

A B C D	Structures : Steel : Painting : Inspection
B C D A	Steel : Painting : Inspection : Structures
C D A B	Painting : Inspection : Structures : Steel
D A B C	Inspection : Structures : Steel : Painting

Rotated indexing

<u>A</u> B C D	<u>Structures</u> : Steel : Painting : Inspection
A <u>B</u> C D	Structures : <u>Steel</u> : Painting : Inspection
A B <u>C</u> D	Structures : Steel : <u>Painting</u> : Inspection
A B C <u>D</u>	Structures : Steel : Painting : <u>Inspection</u>

SLIC indexing

A B C D	Structures : Steel : Painting : Inspection
A C D	Structures : Painting : Inspection
A D	Structures : Inspection
B C D	Steel : Painting : Inspection
C D	Painting : Inspection
D	Inspection.

9.4 PRECIS indexing system

The earlier parts of this chapter have considered some of the general issues relating to pre-coordinate indexes. It is now time to turn to a case study, and this section is devoted to one indexing system in rather more depth. The PRECIS indexing system is a set of procedures for producing index entries which in theoretical terms represents an advance outstanding for its highly formularized approach to citation order and reference, or added entry, generation. The student should learn from this more detailed study of the one system, some of the characteristics of pre-coordinate indexing systems in general.

PRECIS is an acronym for *PRE*served *C*ontext *I*ndexing *S*ystem. To date PRECIS indexing has been used in:

● indexes to monographs and periodicals, such as the *British national bibliography, British education index* and the *Australian national bibliography*
● indexes to audio-visual materials, e.g. audio-visual materials for higher education, film catalogues
● indexes to library catalogues, e.g. the subject index of the East Sussex public libraries

PRECIS has also been tested in various experimental indexes and pilot projects. Some of these pilot projects have been: an index to scientific report literature; indexes to public records; an index to monographs and microdocuments on housing; an index to musical scores and monographs on music; and an index to research projects in environmental studies.

Although PRECIS indexing principles have found applications in various sectors of indexing practice, the potential areas of application are far from being exhausted. The firm theoretical analysis underlying the procedures recommends PRECIS indexing as a serious candidate in any consideration of indexing methods. To date probably the most important application of PRECIS indexing is in the subject index to the *British national bibliography.* This tool has provided both a very significant testing ground for the techniques, and also an influential disseminator of the methods.

The lineage of PRECIS indexing

PRECIS indexing has roots in faceted classification, and provides an exemplary illustration of the association and common ground between alphabetical indexing and classification. In order to trace this connection, we will start with the Library Association Conference that was called in 1963 with the objective of reviewing the need for a new general classification scheme. Existing general classification schemes were acknowledged to suffer from:

- lack of specificity
- lack of currency
- poor hospitality
- lack of predictability
- unsuitability for machine manipulation.

Following this early conference, the NATO/Classification Research Group research project undertook investigations into the nature of a proposed new general classification scheme. The project concentrated its efforts towards establishing a system of categories, and devising a scheme of rules for combining individual concepts. Three significant products emerged from the research:

- an outline thesaurus or general system of categories
- a set of relational operators (for relating concepts within a subject) which carried an in-built filing order
- provisional rules for classing, based upon a standard citation order.

Eventually, it came to be recognized that the Classification Research Group's endeavours might be pertinent to the problem of alphabetical indexing. The five steps enumerated as being necessary components of the process of classing a subject needed only slight modification in order to fit an alphabetical indexing environment. These five steps were as follows:

1 Split any compound subject into its component parts.

2 Locate these parts in a thesaurus, and translate the terms or concepts into a notation.

135

3   Determine, from the component parts, the principal concept.

4   Determine the roles of the other components and prefix each piece of notation representing an individual concept accordingly.

5   Set the components down as an ordered string of symbols, according to the filing value of the role operator.

When these five steps have been completed an index string of the following type will result:

C35(5) q24(59)×75(599)v6(54)B27(546)r2

(This is a coding of the subject 'Energy balance in the turbulent mixing layers of a gas'.)

Imagine using such notation for shelf arrangement! Whatever the merits or limitations of the approach for classification practice and theory, it was observed that this type of string showed potential for alphabetical index headings. If the description of the individual components in the heading were translated into terms from an alphabetical controlled indexing language instead of into the notation of a classification scheme a string would result which could form the basis of a set of alphabetical index entries. The role coding could be retained as a means of ordering the components in the string, and serve to indicate which additional entries should be made and how they should be formulated.

The *British national bibliography* MARC Project was under way, and the potential of new research in classification theory was recognized. The BNB MARC Project involved developing a subject indexing technique that could replace the chain indexing used in the traditional production of the *British national bibliography*. The technique selected had to be capable of generating a subject index to the classified sequence in the printed *British national bibliography* and, at the same time, provide alphabetical subject data for storage as part of the BNB MARC files. PRECIS was evolved and adopted by the BNB MARC project, and the fundamental ideas of context dependency, lead terms and the index entry format were developed. The subsequent OSTI (Office for Scientific and Technical Information) PRECIS project was a more concentrated effort to refine PRECIS and make it suitable for operational use in both the *British national bibliography* and other applications. At this stage the ideas were tested on *The sociology of education abstracts*. As a result of these investigations, the manipulation codes were revised and the scheme of operators re-drafted. In 1971 the experimental phase of PRECIS was drawing to a close as the system became operational in the *British national bibliography*. The system was finally settled in 1974, with minor refinements being introduced between 1971 and 1974 in the light of experience. Austin's *PRECIS manual* published in 1974 contains a full explanation of the theoretical background to PRECIS and various of the tests that have been conducted on the system. The manual is essential reading for any indexer who wishes to appreciate fully the intricacies of the system. The second edition of Austin's *PRECIS manual*, published in 1984, adds additional insights into the evolution and application of PRECIS, and Dykstra, M., *PRECIS: a primer*, published in 1985, offers the long-awaited 'idiot's guide' to PRECIS indexing. Various other accounts of PRECIS are available which together treat both practical and theoretical aspects of the system.

PRECIS index entries
In keeping with the acronym, PRECIS is an alphabetical subject indexing system that both presents a 'précis' of the subject content of a document at each entry point, and also displays index terms in context. The index user can enter the index via any of the concepts present in the compound subject, and locate, at that entry point, the full description of the subject. Each index entry has both a lead term and terms conveying context which are displayed in a way that maximizes the information conveyed by the entry. It must be emphasized that PRECIS is a set of procedures for generating index entries and not an indexing language. However, in any application there must be a controlled vocabulary to which the PRECIS routines can be applied. Below are shown the entries that PRECIS indexing would generate in association with the topic 'The training of personnel in India's cotton industries'.

> *Entries*
> 1 India
>   Cotton industries. Personnel. Training
> 2 Cotton industries. India
>   Personnel. Training
> 3 Personnel. Cotton industries. India
>   Training
> 4 Training. Personnel. Cotton industries. India
>
> *References*
> 1 Asia
>   *see also*
>   India
> 2 Industries
>   *see also*
>   Textile industries
> 3 Textile industries
>   *see also*
>   Cotton industries
> 4 Employees *see* Personnel
> 5 Labour *see* Personnel

6 Staff *see* Personnel
7 Workers *see* Personnel
8 Manpower
   see also
      Personnel
9 Education
   see also
      Training

Certain characteristic features of PRECIS index entries and references are evident, and some points to be noted are:

- all entries contain all of the index terms used in the description of the topic
- access is possible via each and any of the index terms
- all terms in the line following the lead term appear in an order that ensures that specific terms are listed first, followed by more general terms
- the subject description is clear in each entry
- index entries usually occupy two lines.

From PRECIS index strings to index entries
All index entries and references in a PRECIS index are derived from an indexing string. This string codifies syntactic relationships, establishes a citation order, and triggers the generation of references for semantic relationships. The role of the string in establishing a citation order for the component parts of each index entry will be considered first. Citation order must be related to the syntactic relationships that are inherent in the subject to be indexed. Syntactic relationships, that is, those relationships that arise from the syntax, are document dependent, and need not be constant. For example, both of the following two topics are comprised of the same component concepts, but the relationships between the concepts are different: 'The assessment of students by teachers', and 'The assessment of teachers by students'.

It is the distinct syntactical relationships in these subjects which are responsible for their being two disparate topics. PRECIS relies upon citation order (sometimes with the support of prepositions) to record syntactical relationships, and to delineate two similar subjects. In order to examine the citation order achieved in PRECIS index entries further it is necessary to examine the procedure for formulating an index string. Seven principal steps lead to the construction of the index string:

1 Identify the elements or concepts of the compound subject that are to be reflected in the index entries. A concept is defined to be a topic matching a PRECIS operator, and may on occasions be a composite subject.

138

2 Express the concepts to be indexed in terms acceptable in the vocabulary to be used in the index. The vocabulary used in conjunction with PRECIS by the *British national bibliography* is split into two sections, one part for Entities (or things) and the other for Attributes (properties of things, e.g. colour, weight; activities of things, e.g. flow, machining; and properties of activities, e.g. slow, turbulent). The terms present in these vocabularies are hierarchically arranged in order to indicate any fundamental generic relationships, and to suggest references that might be made as links between terms. The vocabularies and the hierarchical structure of terms are continually under review. Once terms have been selected they must be examined for the presence of 'foci' and 'differences'. A focus conveys the key or principal notion of a concept. A 'difference' is the adjectival term attached to and limiting a focus. For instance, the subject 'Hibernating animals' contains one focus 'Animals' and one difference 'Hibernating', but other topics such as 'Reinforced concrete bridges' contain two differences 'Reinforced' and 'Concrete', both of which delimit 'Bridges' in some sense.

3 Assign an 'operator' or 'code' to each term identified in Step 2 above. Operators note the role that each term or concept plays in the overall subject. More precise descriptions of the operators appear in the next subsection. Each operator has a filing value which has been designated in order to ensure that terms appear in the index string in an order that will produce a meaningful set of index entries. The order thus determined embodies 'context dependency'; each term in the string sets each successive term in context.

4 Arrange the index terms in an order, in accordance with the filing values of the operators that the terms have been allocated. The end product of this stage will be an index string which encompasses both terms and operators.

5 Speculate as to the index entries that the index string will cause to be generated, and make any necessary adjustments to indexing. In particular note, for example, by ticking them, those terms that merit a turn in the lead position, and those that do not.

6 Insert computer instruction codes in the positions of the operators in the string. These instruction codes convert the operators into machine-readable manipulation codes, and show which terms are to be used as entry terms. The order of terms in the string is retained. This stage marks the end of the indexer's task. The computer has now been provided with the wherewithal to complete the generation of index entries.

7 The computer takes the index string with its machine-readable manipulation codes and creates a series of entries by rotating the component terms with which it has been provided. Each entry has three fundamental positions:

LEAD   Qualifier
Display

This layout, with the lead term being followed by the wider or context-establishing terms on the same line (known as the Qualifier) and narrower terms (the Display) assigned to the second line, becomes particularly significant where, with a different rotation mechanism confusion could result from a change in the order of the indexing terms. The first entry takes the first component of the string as the index term, and leaves the remainder of the string in the Display position. In successive index entries the previous lead term is shunted into the Qualifier position, and the first term in the Display moves into the lead position. This procedure generates entries according to the standard pattern. Sometimes, in the interests of comprehension or helpfulness, modifications to the standard pattern are desirable. Not all of the terms need to be marked as lead terms; this results in the omission of one or more of the entries formed as part of the standard procedure. On other occasions, the order of terms may be adjusted or extra words inserted. These modifications may be enacted by the intervention of the appropriate operator(s). The entries that result from the rotation mechanism have standard layout, punctuation and typography, all of which have been pre-programmed.

Let us apply each of the above seven steps, in turn, to a specific example. The topic to be indexed is: 'The diagnosis of heart disease in man by electrocardiography'. The first two steps are to recognize the individual concepts present in the topic, and to express them in the terms available in the controlled vocabulary. These terms might be:

Man
Heart
Acute diseases
Diagnosis
Electrocardiography

The third step sees the operators assigned. First, an action term is located. Here 'Diagnosis' is an action term, and so the operator for an action term is assigned to 'Diagnosis', viz:

(2) Diagnosis

The object of the action or the key system is next sought and coded (1). Hence:

(1) Man

'Heart' is part of the key system 'Man', and a part is designated by (p), so

(p) Heart

and likewise:

(p) Acute diseases

Only 'Electrocardiography' remains, which is easily identified as the technique; techniques or agents are coded (3), and so

(3) Electrocardiography

Next, the organization of terms according to the filing value of their operators gives an indexing string:

(1) Man (p) Heart (p) Acute diseases
(2) Diagnosis
(3) Electrocardiography

Step 5 involves the designation of lead terms. If all terms merit a lead entry then:

(1) Man ✓ (p) Heart ✓ (p) Acute diseases ✓
(2) Diagnosis ✓
(3) Electrocardiography ✓

Once computer instruction codes have been inserted in Step 6, the computer will generate the following index entries:

1 MAN
   Heart. Acute diseases. Diagnosis. Electrocardiography
2 HEART. Man
   Acute diseases. Diagnosis. Electrocardiography
3 ACUTE DISEASES. Heart. Man
   Diagnosis. Electrocardiography
4 DIAGNOSIS. Acute diseases. Heart. Man
   Electrocardiography
5 ELECTROCARDIOGRAPHY. Diagnosis. Acute diseases. Heart.
   Man

Operators and codes
Operators, also called role operators, are numbers and letters which are assigned to terms in a string to specify their grammatical function or role within that string. Operators are used to designate the syntactical components of a string. Built into each operator are sets of instructions to the computer which regulate where the term must appear in the printed entries generated from the string, typefaces, and necessary punctuation. The PRECIS operators and codes are shown in figure 9.2.

Fig. 9.2 PRECIS operators and codes

SCHEMA OF OPERATORS

Primary operators

Environment of core concepts	0	Location
Core concepts	1	Key system
		Thing when action not present.
		Thing towards which an action is directed e.g. object of transitive action, performer of intransitive action.
	2	Action: Effect of action
	3	Performer of transitive action *(agent, instrument)*; Intake: Factor
Extra-core concepts	4	Viewpoint-as-form: Aspect
	5	Selected instance. *e.g. study region, sample population*
	6	Form of document: Target user

Secondary operators

Coordinate concepts	f	'Bound' coordinate concept
	g	Standard coordinate concept
Dependent elements	p	Part: Property
	q	Member of quasi-generic group
	r	Assembly
Special classes of action	s	Role definer: Directional property
	t	Author-attributed association
	u	Two-way interaction

Note on prefixes to Codes. The codes in the left-hand panel are marked as instructions, as opposed to data, by their preceding symbols. These are shown as dollar signs ($) to reflect current practice in many PRECIS files, but any non-alpha-numeric character will serve the same purpose. The draft version of the *UNIMARC Manual* (referring to PRECIS data in Field 670) states that 'signs used as subfield codes (in UNIMARC: the $) *should be avoided*'.

CODES IN PRECIS STRINGS

Primary codes

Theme interlinks	$x	1st concept in coordinate theme
	$y	2nd/subsequent concept in theme
	$z	Common concept
Term codes*	$a	Common noun
	$c	Proper name (class-of-one)
	$d	Place name

Secondary codes

Differences

Preceding differences (3 characters)

1st and 2nd characters:

$0 Non-lead, space generating
$1 Non-lead, close-up
$2 Lead, space generating
$3 Lead, close-up

3rd character = number in the range 1 to 9 indicating level of difference

Date as a difference	$d	
Parenthetical differences	$n	Non-lead parenthetical difference
	$o	Lead parenthetical difference
Connectives	$v	Downward-reading connectives
	$w	Upward-reading connective

Typographic codes*

$e Non-filing part in italic preceded by comma
$f Filing part in italic preceded by comma
$g Filing part in roman, no preceding punctuation
$h Filing part in italic preceded by full point
$i Filing part in italic, no preceding punctuation

*These codes are also used in the thesaurus

The purpose of the operators and codes can be more fully enumerated than previously. Operators and codes:

(a) Ensure consistency between the index entries produced by different indexers. All entries for the same or similar subjects should have the same or similar citation orders of component single concepts

(b) Help the indexer to avoid indexing omissions by drawing additional concepts to his attention as he seeks to identify concepts that fit each of the operators

(c) Define that which is to be taken to constitute an indexing unit or term, by indicating whether terms should be retained as compound terms or analysed into smaller units, e.g. 'Personnel selection' or 'Personnel' and 'Selection'

(d) Ensure that the components of a heading are cited in such a way as to establish context dependency, and that this citation order once established is retained

(e) Form the basis of the machine manipulation codes, and thus make a contribution to the regulation of the format of the index entries, their typography and punctuation.

In order to understand the citation order that PRECIS indexing advocates it is necessary to examine the function of the operators more closely. This section proceeds to introduce the operators and their functions. No attempt is made to provide any detailed familiarity with the entire range of operators; that would be too ambitious an aim for this modest account. Many of the statements are generalizations, and exceptions have been overlooked in the interests of clarity.

The primary operators are designated by numbers, viz, 0, 1, 2, 3, 4, 5 and 6. Their function is to denote the basic concepts of a compound subject. Operators 0, 1, 2, and 3 are used to mark the core concepts and their environment. Every string must commence with one of the operators 0, 1 or 2. The primary operators determine the fundamental citation order for the string, and are cited ordinally. Operator 1 introduces the key system, which must be an entity (or a thing). Operator 2 precedes actions and phenomena which imply actions or the effect of an action on the system (for example, road safety, diseases). In general, the entity upon which the action is being performed should be labelled as the key system. Operator 3 introduces the performers of transitive actions, whether they be things or phenomena. These three operators are demonstrated in the following string which provides the basis for the indexing of the topic: 'Tractors for the transportation of lumber'.

(1) Lumber
(2) Transportation
(3) Tractors

Operator 4 introduces any statement of viewpoint. Thus, a work on 'The sociological perspectives of industrial relations in Great Britain' might be coded in the following manner:

(0) Great Britain
(2) Industrial relations
(4) Sociological perspectives

Operators 0 and 5 may be used to designate a location. The operator 0 introduces a place name where the relational link between a locality and any following concept is simply one of geographical constraint. The operator 5, on the other hand, introduces terms such as 'Study regions' or 'Study examples', as exemplified in the string below:

(1) Book trade
(2) Management
(5) Study regions   (q) Germany

Here Germany, the name of the place, is specifically cited as merely the area in which the researches were conducted into the nature of a general phenomenon. The last of the primary operators, 6, prefaces terms which describe either the form (e.g. that it is a dictionary or bibliography) or the target audience (e.g. that it is intended for nurses or midwives) of the document.

In addition to the primary operators, PRECIS employs a number of secondary operators, as listed in figure 9.2. Dependent elements are signalled by p, q and r. These are used to indicate a concept that is dependent on a preceding concept. Operator p, for example, is used to designate a part, or a property of, a thing or action. An example is:

(1) bicycles   (p) wheels

q is used to preface a member of a quasi-generic group, as in, for example:

(1) libraries   (p) stock   (q) non-book materials

where 'stock' is the quasi-generic group, and 'non-book materials' is one member of that quasi-generic group.

The next set of secondary operators are the coordinate concept operators, f and g. Both f and g cater for the insertion of co-ordinate concepts which share a mutual relationship with some other components in the string. An example is:

(1) pets   (q) cats $V & (g) dogs   (2) training

where 'dogs' is a coordinate concept to 'cats'.

The final two operators are s and t. Labelled as operators for special classes of action they are the most sophisticated operators. They can be used to permit the inclusion of words that aid in the clarification of the

144

relationships between concepts in entries. For example, the s in the following string allows appropriate linking words to be introduced to coordinate concepts in a clear manner:

Subject
The role of drama in behaviour therapy

String
(2) Behaviour therapy
(s) Role $V of $W in
(3) Drama

Entries
1   Behaviour therapy
       Role of drama
2   Drama
       Role in behaviour therapy

In addition to the operators, there are a number of codes. Again, there are primary and secondary codes. All codes carry instructions to the computer. The primary codes account for two positions in the nine-position computer-manipulation code that precedes each term. The secondary and typographic codes do not precede terms but are placed after or among them as, for example, when terms consist of more than one word and each word requires separate computer manipulation.

The differencing codes cater for terms which consist of more than one word, such as Professional education, Steel tubes. Compound terms can be entered under their first words without further refinement, provided we do not require entries under the second word in the term. Differencing is a method for providing entries under words other than the first in a compound term. Two pieces of jargon are useful. All terms include a 'focus', which determines the general class to which the term refers, e.g. Timber, Tube. The focus is a noun. The focus may be qualified by one or more differences. Differences make a focus more specific, e.g. Powdered, in Powdered milk. Differences are often adjectives, but may also be other words or phrases which serve the same logical purpose. If, for example, we wished to produce index entries for 'Skimmed milk', the coding and entries might be:

String
(1)   Milk $21 Skimmed

Entries
(1)   Milk
        Skimmed milk
(2)   Skimmed milk

$21 is the code for a 'lead' space generating preceding difference, which is a first-level difference (i.e. it applies directly to the focus). If, however, we wished to close up a difference, the code $31 would be appropriate. For example:

String
(1) Milk $31 Butter

Entries
1   Milk
         Buttermilk
2   Buttermilk

An example that uses a wider range of differences, including second-level differences (differences that apply to another difference) is:

Subject
Quick-frozen garden peas

String
(1) Peas $21 Garden $21 Frozen $32 Quick-

Entries
1   Peas
         Quick-frozen garden peas
2   Garden peas
         Quick-frozen garden peas
3   Frozen peas
         Quick-frozen garden peas
4   Quick-frozen peas
         Quick-frozen garden peas

The other differencing operator, d, introduces dates.

The other codes include theme interlinks and term codes. Theme interlinks are designated by $x, $y and $z. These allow coordinate topics within a complex subject to be coded and the concepts of one coordinate subject to be distinguished from those of another. The term codes, $a, $c, $d, are used to indicate certain special kinds of terms. Connectives can be prefaced by $v and $w. By this means prepositions can be inserted in strings.

It is worth reiterating that the chief effect of the coding of terms with operators lies in the arrangement of terms in the final index entries. The intention is always to achieve a clear and complete subject description and provide entries at each of the reasonable access points. The student might be reassured to recognize that this type of fundamental analysis of a subject need be conducted only once for each subject entering the indexing system. Once a subject has been treated it is assigned an SIN

(Subject Indicator Number) and when the subject next occurs, the indexer need only notify the SIN in order to trigger the mechanism for printing the complete set of index entries.

Semantic relationships and thesaural aspects

No semantically related or synonymous terms are incorporated into the one PRECIS entry. The discussion above on operators and syntactic relationships assumes that semantic relationships will be treated by a separate mechanism. Semantic relationships are document independent and relatively invariant. They represent the relationships that would be recognized by any student of a subject. For example, that Topology is a branch of Mathematics is generally agreed and unlikely to be subject to change. Semantic relationships must be indicated by *see* and *see also* references of the type incorporated into the PRECIS index entries and references shown on pp.137–138.

References are generated from an index string but as a distinct operation from the printing of index entries. When a string has been constructed by an indexer it is examined for any new terms. For each term entering the vocabulary a record is constructed in the computer-held file which contains one or more of:

- reference indicator number (RIN) which uniquely identifies an address
- the term assigned to that address
- in the case of a target term, one or more reference-generating codes, followed by the RIN of a referred-from term. The code indicates the relationship between the target term and the referred-from term, and the type of reference that is to be printed (i.e. *see* or *see also*).

Thus, the three records corresponding to the term exemplified on pp.137–138 might contain the following data:

```
0003514   Industries
0010464   Textile industries   $o   0003514
005920x   Cotton industries    $o   0010464
```

In this display the addresses appear in the first column, and are followed by the index term, and next comes the reference-generating code, and then, the RIN of the related term.

The computer-held records for each term will cause the generation of references. Using the same example, references are generated in accordance with the following procedure:

1 The presence of the RIN for 'Cotton industries' in a string causes the computer to locate the RIN in its store and record the target term stored in association with the RIN.

2 The computer interprets the reference-generating codes held at this address.

3 The computer then proceeds to the address after the reference-generating code and extracts and prints the referred-from term. This procedure might cause a reference of the type:

Textile industries
see also
Cotton industries

to be printed.

4 A repeat of this sequence of operations will be responsible for creating other references, as shown on pp.137—138.

It is possible to suppress references and to omit steps in a hierarchy.

PRECIS and online searching

As indicated earlier in this chapter, PRECIS indexing is primarily designed to support the production of printed indexes. However, experiments with PRECIS indexing strings have demonstrated the advantages of a pre-coordinate indexing system in online searching. MARC records, including PRECIS data, have been searched in online searching environments. An early online information-retrieval system using PRECIS was the Ontario Educational Research Information System (ONTERIS). Online subject retrieval with PRECIS is available through BLAISE-LINE. PRECIS is also used in the National Film Board of Canada's FORMAT system, which is stored in UTLAS.

Each online retrieval system using PRECIS has used different search software, but they all use PRECIS in a similar way. Each term (or each word in a compound term) in a PRECIS string is individually searchable, and may be combined with Boolean operators, etc. Thus, a post-coordinate search is performed on pre-coordinate terms. This means that a number of PRECIS strings may match the one search statement. With suitable software, these strings can be displayed, and a more precise search can proceed based upon the strings. For example, if a search is made on the terms 'teachers' and 'attitudes', the following strings would emerge:

1 $zl1030$a teachers
  $zpl030$a attitudes

2 $zl1030$a primary schools
  $zpl030$a teachers $21 part-time
  $zsl030$a attitudes $v of $w to
  $z31030$a administration

3 $zl1030$a universities
  $zpl030$a students
  $zsl030$a attitudes $v of $w to
  $z3kl31$a teachers

4 $z11030$a children
  $zpl030$a health $w of
  $zsl030$a attitudes $v of $w to
  $z31030$a teachers

5 $z11030$a teachers
  $z51030$a attitudes $v of $w to
  $z31030$a librarians

6 $z11030$a students $21 black
  $zpl030$a attitudes $w of
  $zs0030$a influence $v of $w on
  $z31030$a teachers

Clearly, there is no further need for manipulation of the strings, as in a printed index. There is scope for more investigation into the value and effectiveness of PRECIS in an online environment.

Pre-coordinate indexing has been introduced in this chapter. The essential nature of pre-coordinate indexing has been identified and the importance of pre-coordinate indexing in producing printed indexes and its potential in online retrieval from computer-based databases have been considered. The future importance of pre-coordinate indexing depends upon the fate of printed indexes, and upon recognition of the value of pre-coordination of concepts in computerized information retrieval.

Chapter 10

THE USE OF ABSTRACTING AND INDEXING DATA

This chapter presents a brief overview of some of the applications of indexing and abstracting data. The account makes no pretence of being comprehensive and for a thorough treatment of these areas other texts should be consulted. The objective here is to select representative products from the array of abstracts and index-based services and illustrate how some of the techniques introduced in other parts of this book may be put into practice.

10.1 Primary publications

Both abstracting and indexing data are to be found in association with, or can be created from the text of, primary publications such as books, reports, journal articles, conference proceedings, theses and dissertations. Both printed and electronic versions of documents may be provided with abstracts and/or indexes. The abstracts and indexes in such environments are extremely variable in quality, style and intent.

Abstracts, first, will accompany various learned, technical or scholarly contributions. A typical application is in juxtaposition to articles in scholarly periodicals. Abstracts that are incorporated into such publications are provided with one or more of the following objectives in mind:

- to orient the reader who intends to proceed to the remainder of the text
- to act as a summary of the text for the purposes of selection of reading material
- to permit the person needing an overview of a subject area, e.g. a teacher or manager, to keep abreast of advances without necessarily scanning entire articles.

Likewise, abstracts are normally required to be submitted together with dissertations, theses and reports. Again, the above three objectives are intended to be fulfilled. For example, an abstract accompanying a report is intended primarily to permit the manager, sponsor or contractee to evaluate a piece of research, and equip him to consider the results, conclusions and recommendations of the work.

Abstracts to be found in primary publications are generally written by the author of the publication that carries the abstract. Some of these abstracts will be edited by, for example, a journal editor, but many will pass into print with little intervention. Too often the author has no clear objective in preparing an abstract other than that he has been instructed to do so by the agency that is about to publish his contribution. Often the abstract is an ill-planned afterthought. Again, all of the advantages and disadvantages of author abstracts which were mentioned in Chapter 2 are applicable.

Indexes are also a feature of some primary publications. Those publications consisting of several contributions are most likely to carry indexes. A research report will not normally be indexed but a book, periodical or conference proceedings might. Most substantial monographs and conference proceedings carry an index which provides access to the concepts explored in the work. Again, these indexes are usually constructed by the author, although sometimes the services of a professional indexer may be employed. Most journals that make any claim to contribute to the established and recorded body of knowledge are provided with indexes to access their contribution. Journals may carry author and subject indexes, together with any appropriate special indexes. The main indexes may cover the articles in the periodical, and perhaps a separate index to book reviews might be justified. Most printed periodical indexes are not distributed with each issue of the periodical but appear in order to cover several issues. Annual indexes are common. Annual indexes over several years may be cumulated to five-yearly or ten-yearly indexes. The indexing data in periodicals are normally controlled by the journal editor or a specialist indexer and hence the indexes should reveal the skills of an indexer who is at least accustomed to indexing. Some editors and indexers for scholarly periodicals are subject experts rather than information experts and this may be reflected by the indexing in the periodical. Indexing practices in periodicals may not adhere to any standard indexing guidelines or principles, but they may reflect the way that a subject expert in the field concerned describes and expects to locate his subject. Indexes in electronic documents such as journals and directories are still in their infancy. So far they have tended to adopt a similar style to the indexes in equivalent printed products.

Abstracts and indexes, then, are present in primary publications. The quality, quantity and function of such data vary considerably.

10.2 Abstracting and indexing journals and bulletins
Printed abstracting and indexing services remain a very economic avenue for the provision of a large number of users with a wide-ranging and reasonably effective reference-retrieval service. The published abstracting and indexing journal probably still retains its prominence as an

information tool in which abstracting and indexing data are used, despite competition from its more fashionable rivals. In-house abstracts bulletins can also hold their own against more selective services, and these will be reviewed later in this section.

Most larger academic and public reference libraries rely to a considerable extent upon printed abstracting and indexing journals as reference-retrieval tools. Special libraries and information centres tend to develop smaller, more topic-centred collections, and hence provide the chief market for abstracting and indexing journals covering the narrower subject fields.

Abstracting journals list, usually within alphabetical subject headings, or in a classified sequence, bibliographical information together with abstracts. Some abstracting journals are published as independent publications, e.g. *Chemical abstracts, Metals abstracts, Library and information science abstracts, Ergonomic abstracts*, whilst other abstracting journals are distributed as a section in a primary periodical. Examples of this latter type are found in *Platinum metals review, Rubber developments* and the *Journal of dentistry*. Other journals often have short reviews or abstracts of new literature such as books, reports and trade literature. Examples of periodicals including these are *Plastics engineering, Welding journal* and *Product finishing*. Abstracting journals vary enormously in scope ranging from vast publications covering an entire discipline, such as *Biological abstracts* or *Chemical abstracts*, to slim volumes centred on a relatively narrow topic such as *Rural recreation and tourism abstracts*.

Indexing journals are more likely than abstracting journals to cover a very broad subject area. The fundamental concept is that they organize an entire area of knowledge. Typical examples are *Applied science and technology index, British education index* and *Current technology index*. As is evident from their name the emphasis is on the indexing data, and indexing journals do not contain abstracts. The bibliographical citations that they contain act merely as access points. These bibliographical data are usually arranged under alphabetical subject headings.

The production of abstracting and indexing services is not centralized. These services are compiled by various organizations very distinct in their nature and functions, but all abstracting and indexing agencies share a common interest in the dissemination of information. Research organizations, professional bodies, government agencies and commercial publishers all engage in the publication of abstracting and/or indexing services. In many countries the national documentation centre is responsible for the production of abstracting and indexing publications. A high proportion of the English-language services are compiled and published in the United States. Publishers in the United States benefit from a larger home market which serves to sustain the production of an information tool. In earlier times, most abstracting and indexing publications used conventional printing technology. Now, most agencies make use of computer printing, indexing and/or formatting. The application of the computer to the production of abstracting and indexing publications has led to the proliferation of large commercially available databases. The access to these databases will be considered in the next sections.

Both abstracting and indexing journals perform two functions. They are intended both as current awareness tools and as retrospective-search tools. In the context of current awareness they help users to keep up to date by offering an organized set of document surrogates. However, their bulk and the comprehensive nature of their coverage make them rather unwieldy and indigestible as current-awareness media. Also, currency is too often a problem. Abstracting journals especially suffer on this score because the preparation and inclusion of abstracts is time-consuming and it is difficult to avoid an unacceptable time lag between the appearance of the original document and its announcement in an abstracting journal. Indexing journals are not hindered by the necessity of providing abstracts, but nevertheless, the larger publications are difficult to keep adequately current. Abstracting and indexing journals then, are perhaps more successful as tools for retrospective searching. Certainly, there have been fewer attempts at alternative provision in this area. An abstracting or indexing publication is a cheap and convenient means of compiling a list of references or bibliography on a given topic. A thorough search through the indexes and issues of the publication over the time period required for the search should reveal an appropriate selection of documents.

Coverage of both abstracting and indexing services varies considerably to the extent that coverage criteria must be based on different premises. Partly on account of the variety of bases for coverage there is significant overlap between the assortment of abstracting and indexing services. A given document may be announced in several secondary publications. Some publications limit coverage by specifying subjects, others list the titles of the periodicals to be scanned, and yet others restrict coverage to certain types of materials, such as patents or dissertations. An item on, for example, 'The management of a chemical plant' might justifiably be listed in both *Management abstracts* and *Chemical abstracts*, and might also merit an entry in *Computer and control abstracts*. Despite this overlap, the other side of the picture is that some materials are covered inadequately or even not at all. In particular, patents, reports and theses often suffer from neglect. Even materials that are relatively thoroughly represented in the abstracting and indexing literature may be covered only in a restricted sense. The depth of coverage of journals, for example, is usually limited; only items regarded as significant may be noted, and shorter items are likely to be omitted.

What is the role of the abstract in an abstracting publication? The abstract is included in order to aid the selection of relevant documents. In a retrospective search, if documents are retrieved on the basis of title alone closer examination may lead to the rejection of documents as being irrelevant. Abstracts permit a more immediate assessment of relevance. Also, a collection of references which includes informative abstracts is a firm basis for a review of a subject area. Abstracts may also contribute to document selection in the current-awareness context. Informative abstracts are particularly useful in permitting a reader to keep abreast of a relatively wide subject area. Unfortunately, the inclusion of abstracts in most services tends to hamper currency. The importance of currency in relation to comprehensiveness and other features of the abstracting publication depends upon the subject area and audience.

Abstracts that are to be published in printed abstracting and indexing journals are often signed in order to endorse the authority of the abstractor. Abstracts may be prepared either by a team of full-time abstractors, or by subject experts who are engaged in the subject in some other capacity, such as research. In-house abstractors are in a better position to achieve consistency in quality and style, whilst subject experts may bring a more informed and critical eye to document analysis. One of the major recurrent problems with volunteer and part-time abstractors is maintaining deadlines; delays in some of the documents covered by the service are almost inevitable.

Indexing data are used both in indexing journals and in the indexes to abstracting journals. Indexing journals, for instance, are usually arranged in one main alphabetical subject order. Supplementary indexes may also offer access by author, title, patent number, trade name, or chemical formula. Equally, abstracting journals must have the entries arranged in a primary sequence. This main sequence may exploit a classification scheme, or group abstracts under alphabetical subject section headings. Here again, additional indexes may offer access from other lead terms. The indexing data in either of these categories of publications serve to provide rapid acces to the records listed in the publication via whatever terms or names are listed in the indexes of the publication. In so doing the indexes act as an organized guide to large sections of the literature of a subject area. Issue and cumulative indexes are to be expected. Five- and ten-yearly cumulative indexes also make retrospective searching less tedious. The time period between the completion of a cycle (e.g. at the end of a volume or a year) and the publication of the associated cumulative indexes should be as short as possible for maximum effectiveness and ease of retrieval.

Abstracting and indexing publications are one of the readily available types of products which incorporate abstracting and indexing data. The reader is urged to examine some of these tools.

The in-house abstracting bulletin is frequently viewed as an alternative dissemination tool to externally produced information services. In concept and content it has much in common with a commercially published abstracting journal. The main distinctions lie in audience and scope. There is no precise definition of an abstracting bulletin, but a bulletin is generally a weekly or monthly current-awareness service containing abstracts of all documents of interest that have passed into the library or information unit during that time. Such bulletins were common prior to computerization and were produced satisfactorily. During the late 1960s many information units experienced two conflicting pressures. They felt that in order to meet the expectations of their audience and sponsors they must widen their coverage, and yet at the same time staff and other resources were becoming more scarce. The solution was computerization. Some bulletins are still produced manually, and some are one of the outputs from a computer-based information-storage and -retrieval system. With computerization some libraries took the opportunity to replace outmoded abstracts bulletins with SDI services, as discussed later.

Abstracting bulletins can form the core of the work of an information unit. The scanning that must be conducted in order to compile an abstracts bulletin may be the primary avenue through which the information staff retain a familiarity with the literature of the unit's subject responsibilities. The preparation of abstracts and their compilation into bulletins to a set schedule, e.g. weekly, may impose a routine upon the working life of the information staff. Often, the abstracting bulletin will be indexed, and the cumulation of the bulletin and its indexing data will constitute the database from which the unit will answer retrospective enquiries. Indeed this database may be a unique collection and organization of data, which may be published or otherwise made available to other interested parties. The bulletin also represents a continuing link with the users of the information unit. Users come to expect the regular appearance of the abstracts bulletin and see this as a positive service that the information unit can be relied upon to supply. The abstracts bulletin will also trigger loans and photocopy requests and hence may have a significant effect on the demands placed upon the circulation and inter-library loans system of the library.

A dilemma facing many librarians and information managers is when an external service should be used, and when it is necessary to take the trouble to create a unique in-house service. Although it has wider implications, this dilemma is evident in the choice and distinction between the in-house abstracting bulletin and the published, commercially available abstracting or indexing journal. The external service can replace an inefficient internal service, provide a totally new service which otherwise could not be offered or augment an existing successful service. In differentiating between the functions of the two categories of service some factors are generally taken into consideration.

1 *Costs* Costs are obviously a crucial factor, although absolute costs are not usually relevant. The cost of an external service can be easily agreed, but the costs associated with an internal service are more difficult to identify. They are likely to involve both staff and materials components, and it may not be the absolute costs of these components, but rather the actual availability of staff and materials that is more crucial.

2 *Staffing* The production of an internal abstracts bulletin requires the skills of expert abstractors with subject appreciation. External services may be in a better position to make efficient use of abstractors and subject experts. However, experienced information staff can make a more positive contribution to an organization than the mere purchase of external information tools.

3 *Coverage* Any service, external or in-house, must match the interests of the users of the library. It is an unfortunate fact that many external services cannot hope to mirror the interests of a specific organization (except possibly with more specialized products than a general abstracts bulletin). Few libraries achieve complete coverage from one external information tool. In considering coverage all of the comments previously made concerning the coverage criteria of abstracting and indexing publications need to be taken into account.

4 *Currency* The relative currency of external and in-house services must be considered. Often it is this factor which is pre-eminent in a decision to provide an in-house bulletin. The intercession of the external agency places a further link in the chain between author and end-user, and hence must increase the likelihood of delay.

5 *Feedback and user relations* An in-house bulletin offers a more tailored product to the library's users and may serve to cement firm relationships with the library's personnel. Feedback is also an important element in the satisfactory operation of a current awareness service. Feedback helps the compiler of the information tool to modify the tool in accordance with the needs of its clientele. The chain between abstracting publication producer and user may be unacceptably long and there is usually too little communication between the two

Similar, but appropriately adjusted considerations, must be taken into account when considering whether to build an in-house database or to use an external database, and in deciding whether to produce any of the printed products, such as a current awareness service, that can be extracted from such a database.

10.3 Databases
Catalogues, files, lists of borrowers, and indexes are all, in a sense, types of databases. The abstracting and indexing publications mentioned previously constitute a type of database. All comprise a series of related

and similarly formatted records. However, the product to be considered in this section is a computer stored database. Again, within this specialized set of databases there are two categories of concern to librarians and information workers: those which the library is responsible for creating, and those that are accessed by the library but whose compilation is beyond the control of the library.

In-house databases may be constructed with the aid of text retrieval packages to cover a plethora of different applications. These might broadly be grouped into administrative, financial, legal, manufacturing, marketing, personnel, and scientific and engineering. Examples within these categories can range from databases on credit history, project control and planning, and skills, to databases on product descriptions. Abstracts are most likely to occur in bibliographic applications, but various other types of summaries may emerge in other databases. There are between one and two hundred text retrieval packages available on the European and American markets. The first packages were available in the early 1970s and ran on mainframe computers. The early 1980s saw the advent of more widely available microcomputers and microcomputer software. The availability of microcomputer-based systems offered opportunities to create computer databases that were previously not available to organizations that had small budgets and a requirement for only a relatively small database. Figure 10.1 gives some examples of mainframe, minicomputer, and microcomputer text retrieval packages that are available in the United Kingdom.

Fig. 10.1 Some examples of text retrieval packages

Package . *Mainframe/minicomputer*	*Suppliers*
ADLIB	LMR Computer Services
ADP/3RIP	ADP Network Services Ltd.
ASSASSIN 6	Imperial Chemical Industries, Agricultural Division
BASIS	Battelle Memorial Institute
CAIRS	Leatherhead Food Research Association
DOCU/MASTER	TSI International (UK) Ltd.
INFO	Doric Computer Systems Ltd./Henco Software Inc.
INQUIRE	Infodata Systems Inc.
SEARCH	BRS
STATUS	AERE Harwell

Fig. 10.1 continued

Package Microcomputer	Suppliers
AQUILA	Kent-Barlow Publications Ltd.
CARDBOX	Business Simulations Ltd.
DOCUMATE PLUS	Ortho Code Corporation
FRONTRUNNER	Decision Technology
GOLDEN RETRIEVER	CLASS
INMAGIC-Micro	Head Computers Ltd.
LIBRARIAN	Eurotec Consultants Ltd.
MICRO-CAIRS	Leatherhead Food Research Association
MICRO-STATUS	AERE Harwell
MIKRO-POLYDOC	Norwegian Centre for Informantics

The librarian may encounter external databases in a variety of contexts. It is possible to purchase or lease the machine-readable version of the database and to process the database locally. In this way the contents of the database may be integrated into the other products of the information service. Alternatively, the librarian may wish to purchase one of the wide range of products that other processors or generators may be stripping from the tape. The special librarian is possibly more likely to be engaged in tape-processing, or word-processing, whereas the products in the information market-place may find buyers amongst special, academic and public libraries, and indeed amongst the users themselves. Whatever his concern with databases the librarian must recognize these as an important product which incorporates abstracting and indexing data.

External databases can be partitioned into two major categories: bibliographic and non-bibliographic or full-text databases. The librarian is preoccupied with bibliographic databases, and indeed these often contain both abstracting and indexing data. Non-bibliographic databases obviously need access points, and must contain indexing data, but probably do not contain abstracts and references. Those non-bibliographic databases of primary concern to the librarian are those which are available through online search systems which impinge upon the information world. These are the publicly available non-bibliographic information databases or data banks. They store the directory-type data to which a library has traditionally attempted to provide access. Such databases concentrate in the areas of business and economics, social sciences and education, and science and technology. In all instances these databases comprise a series of records, but the records are likely to contain facts and figures rather than document representations. Figure 10.2 shows some full-text databases and data banks.

Fig. 10.2 Some full-text databases and data banks

Database	Producer	Host
Company and business information		
ICC British Company Directory	ICC	Dialog
European Kompass Online	Reed International	Reed International
MAGIC	Datasolve	Datasolve
Jordans	Jordan Information Services	Jordan Information Services/ Pergamon-Infoline
MARS	Predicasts	Dialog
Key British Enterprises	Dun & Bradstreet	Pergamon-Infoline
BIS Informat	BIS	Pergamon-Infoline
Textline	Finsbury Data Services	Finsbury Data Services
Dun's Market Identifiers	Dun & Bradstreet	Dialog
EXSTAT	Extel Statistical Services Ltd	Extel Statistical Services Ltd
PTS International Forecasts	Predicasts Inc.	Dialog
BI/Data Time series	Business International Corporation	Dialog
MINTEL Market Intelligence Reports	MINTEL	Datasolve
News and current affairs		
Newsline	Finsbury Data Services	Finsbury Data Services
Newsearch	Information Access Company	Dialog/Mead Data Control
World Reporter	Datasolve Ltd.	Datasolve Ltd.
Scientific and technical		
Fine Chemicals Directory	Fraser Williams (Scientific Systems) Ltd.	Fraser Williams (Scientific Systems) Ltd.
Pharmaprojects Online	V & O Publications Ltd.	Datastar
Agrochemicals Databank	Royal Society of Chemistry	Datastar
DETEQ	DECHEMA	STN International
Kirk-Othmer Online	Wiley Electronic Publishing	BRS/Datastar
Encyclopedia of Polymer Science and Engineering	Wiley Electronic Publishing	BRS/Datastar
General directories		
American Men and Women of Science	R.R. Bowker	Dialog
Encyclopedia of Associations	Gale Research Company	Dialog
Ulrich's International Periodicals Directory	R.R. Bowker	Dialog
Marquis Who's Who	Marquis Who's Who Inc.	Dialog

Bibliographic databases tend to form the central topic of concern for most librarians, and they illustrate the application of both abstracting and indexing data. Bibliographic databases include abstracting and indexing data. These data are very similar to those present in abstracting and indexing publications, and perform the same type of function. The main distinction between the role of the data in the two different environments lies in the rather differing circumstances under which abstracting and indexing data may be accessed. We will return to the access to databases later.

Most bibliographic databases evolved from a parent abstracting or indexing publication. The content of the database and its indexing policies are usually still coloured by the associated printed product. The database may, as a result of its parentage, be handicapped by features that are not suited to computerized retrieval. Coverage may at one extreme be too universal and, at the other, too specialized. Access points may be unsophisticated and derive at least partly from the subject categories used in the printed version. Update is incremental and may be slow, and pricing policies show evidence of the presence of a supporting printed product.

There are a large number of databases from which information products may be derived or which may be accessed online. The earlier and better established databases were primarily in the subject areas of science and technology, but emphasis is shifting in favour of business, financial and commercial databases.

The scope of coverage of databases varies considerably. Some databases are very all-embracing in their coverage and attempt to provide comprehensive coverage of entire disciplines. CHEMABS, BIOSIS Previews, and INSPEC might be numbered amongst these. Other databases also have extensive but slightly less ambitious coverage policies. ERIC is a good example of such a database, covering most of education. There are also smaller, more specialized databases. These are likely to be less well known and familiar only to other specialists in the same area. TITUS for textiles, and OCEANIC for oceans might be mentioned in this context. Other databases use criteria other than subject as the basis of selection. Comprehensive Dissertation Abstracts, from Xerox University Microfilms, is a database geared to covering dissertations on any subject. WPI, from Derwent Publications, concentrates on providing access to the patent literature. Databases may be compiled by one organization or by several geographically distinct units acting cooperatively. For this reason, amongst others, the database and its products may be available in different formats in different countries.

A database has no value in itself. It must be accessible. One of the most important advances achieved by the introduction of the computer into the field of bibliographic databases was the variety of products that can be generated from one set of indexing and abstracting data. An array of products may be derived from the database, and each service can be tailored to match a precise market. Typical database products include:

- selective dissemination of information (SDI)
- group SDI
- standard SDI
- online SDI
- printed abstracting and indexing journals and their indexes
- batch retrospective searching (e.g. bibliographies)
- online retrospective searching
- tape (or disk) services (i.e. buy or lease tapes or disks)
- review services
- thesauri
- classification schemes
- lists of journals covered
- reports (of tests, evaluations and practice)
- computer software

In making use of any of the products of databases it is important to appreciate the limitations of the database. Coverage and overlap must be considered, especially in the light of the overlap that will inevitably exist between databases. The length of the period covered by the database is also pertinent. Few databases cover more than the last 20 years.

10.4 Online searching

The possibility of conducting an interactive search of a bibliographic or non-bibliographic database is afforded in a computerized information-storage and -retrieval system. An online and interactive search must be performed via an online search terminal. This terminal must comprise two elements: a device for the user to communicate with the computer, and a second device through which the computer may communicate with the user. The device through which the user codes messages is usually a keyboard similar to the keyboard on a typewriter. The computer's responses may either be displayed on a visual display unit on something akin to a television screen, or printed with the intercession of a printer. The visual display unit is arguably easier to read and more flexible in developing search statements, yet the printer has the advantage that a permanent record of the search is generated. The terminal must be connected to a computer on which the databases that the user wishes to interrogate are mounted. This connection is some type of telecommun-ications link, and may well be part of the public telecommunications network. The computer which holds the required databases may be in the same building as the terminal or anything up to several thousand miles distant. Thus online searching can be conducted on an in-house information-retrieval system mounted on a local computer, or on an external system. In this section we will concentrate on the publicly available online systems and neglect the in-house systems. Comments that are relevant to in-house systems are to be found in other sections in this chapter.

Online access to bibliographic databases offers access to the same type of information that could be retrieved from parallel abstracting and indexing publications. Online access via a large online system which makes several databases available has some advantages over the printed abstracting and indexing journal, although both avenues have a place. Whatever the future may hold, currently quests for information that can be sought under a single simple heading in a subject index are usually best performed in a hard-copy version of the database. Online access comes into its own for the type of search that has been introduced in Chapters 8 and 9. Searches where online access is likely to prove particularly fruitful include:

(a) searches where flexibility is important and it is useful to be able to change or modify search strategy in the light of knowledge gained during the search process
(b) searches which are difficult to perform in a printed index due to the terms that best express the topic not being accepted terms in the language of the index, or in order to be sufficiently precise the search must be stated as a complex logical statement linking a number of index terms
(c) searches where an extensive bibliography is the anticipated output
(d) searches where according to some viewpoint machine searching is the cheapest alternative. The cost of online searching is altering continually, and the economics of the systems must be reassessed from time to time
(e) searches where machine searching offers a wider range of information tools than are available in the library's normal stock of printed indexes.

If, in the light of consideration of the above factors, an online search is deemed appropriate the information officer will proceed to conduct or initiate an online search. With a clear idea of the request and the parameters to be considered in assessing document relevance the searcher will select an online system and a database that can be accessed via the chosen system. The search will proceed as illustrated in Chapter 8. The search statement is post-coordinate in nature, and is a series of index terms linked by search logic. Most of the major systems use Boolean search logic as the main search logic. The computer can be relied upon to supply prompts and additional information to aid in the formulation of the search statement although in the interests of economy it is normal practice to have considered some of the possible refinements of the search statement prior to logging on. The search proceeds as the user introduces a series of commands, and the computer responds to the commands.

10.5 Current-awareness services

Many current-awareness services exploit indexing and abstracting data. Some of the services previously discussed have a current-awareness function. This section mentions other current-awareness services. Current-awareness services are those information services whose primary objective is to keep information users abreast of advances in their field. Any current-awareness service involves the collection of document surrogates and their arrangement and dispatch to users who can be expected to be interested in the associated document. Some current-awareness services make use of abstracts, others use indexing data, and others need both types of data. A KWIC index or other title index may be a simple form of current-awareness service. Titles of recent documents are merely input to a computer which rearranges them into the standard format for a KWIC index. As many copies of the index as are necessary can be printed. Titles can also form the basis of other current-awareness listings, and are perhaps most commonly encountered in 'titles lists' or titles bulletins. These are lists of titles arranged under subject headings or classification numbers, and distributed at appropriate regular intervals. The contents of such bulletins may or may not be indexed. Contents page bulletins which comprise copies of contents pages of periodicals collated and dispatched to users are also reliant upon titles. These, however, rarely call upon the skills of an indexer or abstractor. Most current-awareness services make some use of both abstracting and indexing data. If documents are worthy of abstracting it is worthwhile to index them so that they can be retrieved at a future date.

Although a current-awareness service that incorporates indexing and abstracting data is an effective way of building a database for later retrieval, as well as catering for current-awareness provision, abstracting and indexing are time-consuming processes. There are some environments in which the delay necessary to abstract and index a document would be unacceptable. Here other possibilities must be explored.

Current-awareness services can be generated either in-house by a local organization for its direct clientele, or as one of the products of an external commercially-available database. In either of these environments selective dissemination of information (SDI) services are an important component in a current-awareness publication programme.

SDI is a current-awareness service geared towards the individual. Each person receives a unique set of document notifications which should coincide with his special interests. This type of product is usually achieved via a computer-based information system. It is difficult to remember the special interests of more than a few people, and hence rather taxing to provide SDI manually to more than a handful of users. Documents entering an SDI system are abstracted and assigned a coded document pattern consisting of linked index terms. These terms may be drawn from text by a computer, or assigned from a controlled language by an indexer. Each document pattern is compared with each of a series of user-interest profiles. Each user to be served by the system has his interests encoded in a profile consisting of a linked series of index terms. These terms must be selected in the same way, or from the same language as the terms used to describe documents. An abstract or other document notification is sent to the user if there is a given quality of match between the document coding and the interest-profile coding.

The user-interest profile is the core of the SDI system. Profiles may be constructed by the end-user, his information officer or other intermediary, or a specialist employed by the service vendor. Profiles are based on the user's statement of interests. One way of drawing out such a statement is to request the completion of a profile search form. These forms usually provide space for the user or his agent to enter: the topics to be covered; the keywords that might be pertinent to those topics; and ten or so titles of papers known to be relevant. From these data a formalized search profile which uses the language and logic of the SDI system may be formulated. The search profile will consist of: (a) a list of terms representing the users' interests; and (b) a statement of the logical conditions required for a match that will trigger the printing of a notification. Thus, an SDI search profile is based on index terms and their coordination, and relies upon many of the principles of post-coordinate indexing. The quality of the profile is crucial in the operation of an SDI system. The output from an SDI system is a number of document surrogates in some printed format such as cards or computer printout.

There are four main groups of providers of SDI services: local libraries, large database producers, national libraries and online systems operators. Many local special libraries undertake to provide an SDI service for their users.

There are many organizations that produce in-house current-awareness services. Many of these services are now made available through local area networks within organizations, which are used to make information available to the individual at his workplace. For instance, Rolls-Royce operate a network of 300 terminals, using IBM STAIRS software. Unilever has a network using VIEWDECO software, and at the Atomic Energy Research Establishment, Harwell, there is a network using STATUS software. Increasingly such organizations are using data extracted from external databases in their own databases and current-awareness services. For example, Fisons and Bush Boake Allen both use secondary sources to supplement in-house scanning.

164

SDI can also be acquired direct from some of the large database producers and suppliers. Some of the SDI services on the market are listed below:

SDI	Database	Supplier
ASCA	Science, social sciences, arts and humanities citation indexes	Institute for Scientific Information
COMPENDEX	COMPENDEX	Engineering Index Inc.
INSPEC(SDI)	INSPEC	Institution of Electrical Engineers
UKCIS(SDI)	Chemical abstracts etc	UKCIS

Another major group of SDI suppliers are national libraries. CAN/SDI is possibly the best example of a national SDI service. The service exploits 25 databases ranging across the following disciplines: agriculture, biology, chemistry, medicine, social sciences, education, and science and technology. CAN/SDI is now run cooperatively by five centres and users are to be found in industry, universities, government and hospitals throughout Canada, and to a lesser extent other countries. Australia, Belgium and Denmark also run SDI programmes from a national library. The British Library has responsibility for an SDI service extracted from the MEDLARS database.

Some of the online systems operators also market SDI. This is usually online SDI, unlike most of the other SDI products. With online SDI instead of receiving printed notifications at regular intervals the user has the opportunity to save an SDI profile in the computer store and retrieve and use the profile to search for additional material on specified databases at intervals. DIALOG SDI, for example, gives an automatic printout of appropriate references every time that certain databases are updated. DATA-STAR also offers an online SDI service which permits databases to be searched for new relevant information as they are updated each month.

SDI has proved popular but expensive. Hence some cheaper options for providing SDI to groups of users with similar interests have been explored. Group SDI operates with profiles that match the interests of a group of individuals, such as the personnel of a research department or of a university teaching department. The profile is less specific than the profile for one persons's interests, but the cost of the service is spread between a number of users. Commercial SDI service producers also market what might be described as Standard SDI. A number of set profiles are searched regularly, and subscribers, instead of drafting their own profile select one of the pre-determined profiles. Examples of standard SDI services are: Card-a-lerts, marketed by Engineering Index Inc., ASCA Topics marketed by the Institute for Scientific Information, and INSPEC Topics sold by the Institution of Electrical Engineers.

10.6 Optical disks

Optical disks of various kinds are merely an additional way in which to store and make available databases or sections of databases. There are various different kinds of optical videodisks, including both analog and digital disks, and disks that are read-only (ROM) or write-once-read-many (WORM). The technology is still developing and it is anticipated that the future will bring the erasable optical disk. All disks currently on the market are not erasable once data have been encoded upon them. The optical disk, then, has limited applications as a computer storage medium where it is necessary to be able to erase data and re-use the storage for other data, but has great potential for the development of the optical or electronic publishing industry. Publishers can deliver machine-readable databases direct to customers such as libraries, companies, home users, schools and financial institutions. The database on optical disk can be sold in the same way as any book or printed publication. The electronic document may be a research paper, a book, a directory, an encyclopedia, a bibliographic database or several of these. The electronic document can be sold to the purchaser for a fixed price or subscription. This contrasts sharply with the pay-as-you-go economics of online access. This pricing strategy may be attractive to both users and database producers, both of whom have the security of a predictable and once-only financial transaction. Some would speculate that optical publishing poses a threat to online information retrieval, and the positions of the online hosts. This, in turn, will affect database producers, and their abstractors and indexers. A more extreme point of view is that optical publishing could affect the entire information collection and dissemination process, and thereby change the size, shape and nature of information markets. Clearly, not all sectors of the information market will be equally affected. Figure 10.3 lists some examples of databases currently available on optical disks. It demonstrates the types of databases that are most amenable to publication on optical disk. Some files are too large to be conveniently stored on one optical disk. For example, one estimate is that nine disks might be necessary to record the complete Excerpta Medica database. Equally, databases such as those covering financial and business topics contain data that change too quickly for them to be amenable to supply in the form of an optical disk that is updated, say, only once every three months. On the other hand, optical disks offer interesting marketing possibilities for small specialist bibliographic databases and directory databases.

Fig. 10.3 Some databases available on optical disks

Database	Producer	Distributor
A-V Online	National Information Centre for Educational Media (US)	Silver Platter Information Inc.
Books in Print Plus	Bowker Electronic Publishing	Silver Platter Information Inc.
CD/Corporate	Corporate Technology Services Inc.	Datext Inc.
Compact Cambridge— Medline	Cambridge Scientific Abstracts	Silver Platter Information Inc.
ERIC	ORI Inc.	Silver Platter Information Inc.
Embase (Excepta Medica)	Elsevier Science Publishing Co.	Silver Platter Information Inc.
InfoTrac	Information Access Company	Silver Platter Information Inc.
LC STM (Library of Congress— Science & Technology)	Horizon Information Services	Silver Platter Information Inc.
LegalTrac	Information Access Company	Silver Platter Information Inc.
OCLC Compact Disk— Reference Package	Online Computer Library Center	Library Systems and Services Inc.
Science Citation Index ˙(Permuterm Subject Index)	Institute for Scientific Information	Silver Platter Information Inc.
Wilson Disc	H.W. Wilson Co.	Silver Platter Information Inc.

Appendix

EDITING AND PROOFREADING

Editing is one of the later, yet vital stages in the preparation of any abstracting or indexing publication. The precise nature and extent of the duties of an editor will vary with the publication under consideration, but an editor always has a common goal. An editor's task is to ensure that within the bounds of the resources available the publication and/or database is of a high standard. Aspects such as the physical production of the publication will be important here, but another very important function of an editor is the achievement of consistency. The various contributions from a number of abstractors and indexers must be melded into an integrated whole. Checks for accuracy are linked with consistency and can be conducted simultaneously, but accuracy checks need not be the prime responsibility of the editor. Some checking, such as that directed towards eliminating minor typographical errors, can, if desirable or convenient, be performed separately from editing. Checking and proofreading require only a minimal appreciation of the content and nature of the publication and less knowledgeable staff can satisfactorily complete these tasks. Nevertheless, checking and proofreading must be overseen by the editor. The advent of computerized systems has, in general, reduced the amount of checking and proofreading that is necessary but it remains important to check that the data that have been entered into the database are accurate. The software package which supports the database creation and maintenance should incorporate some validation checks, but these will not cover things that the computer cannot recognize as being incorrect, such as spelling errors or various minor typing mistakes.

The role of the editor
The individual entries in an abstracting publication or an index must be uniform in content, style and presentation. The editor is responsible for ensuring that a high level of uniformity is achieved in all three respects. The preliminary step towards high quality is usually to set standards concerning certain issues, and to convey these standards to individual abstractors and/or indexers. Contributors may be informed of standards to which they are expected to adhere either by word of mouth or through the agency of formal written instructions. Chapter 3 explores the nature

and content of instructions for abstractors more fully. But the formulation of standards and their commitment to printed form do not mean that they will always be noted. Even the best abstractors and indexers may be subject to sloppy practices and grammatical indiscretions from time to time. Indexers cannot always be relied upon to assign the most appropriate term, or to check for its authorization in a controlled list of terms. Volunteer abstractors and indexers, in particular, generally participate in abstracting and indexing on a part-time basis. Although they frequently have valuable contributions to make in terms of subject expertise their appreciation of the nuances of good abstracting style or appropriate indexing terminology may be lacking. They cannot be expected to retain all of the minute details encoded in abstracting and indexing instructions. Under these circumstances, with volunteer contributors it is obviously advisable to keep instructions to a minimum, and to frame rules that are most likely to coincide with the contributors' normal practices. Citation practices, for example, that coincide with those adopted in journals in the subject area will help the abstractor to be orderly.

Abstracting forms

One very common and straightforward device for guaranteeing at the very least a standard format for abstracting contributions is the abstracting form. These forms usually indicate the major categories of data that should be submitted by an abstractor in respect of each record. This clear display of the components of a record enables both the abstractor and the editor to check, at a glance, that all of the essential elements are present on the form.

Abstracting forms take a variety of different formats and styles and, indeed, are probably best formulated for the application for which they are intended. Nevertheless, most forms provide space for each of the following components:

- bibliographical reference
- text of abstract
- indexing terms
- further information, e.g. availability, language.

Some forms split each of these major categories of information into a closely defined series of sub-categories. Abstracts which are to provide the raw material for input to a computerized information system are usually required to be entered on a form which shows the separate fields in the computer record. These forms may be either paper or VDU screen forms or both, depending upon whether the abstractor has access to a computer terminal. If field codings are printed on the abstracting forms these codings may be inserted by the computer operator at the same time as the main text of the abstract and its indexing is converted to machine-readable form.

We will consider each of the four main components of the record in turn, from the point of view of the attention that they require from the editor.

The bibliographical reference, then, will probably be the area where it is essential to achieve consistency in the interests of being able to compare one record with another. Consistency may be facilitated by splitting the reference or citation section of a form into categories which are labelled with the names of the   bibliographical details that are required for a complete reference. Possible sub-categories which may aid the less experienced abstractor might be labelled as: authors' surnames, authors' initials, title of the document, translation of title, journal title, page numbers.

The text of the abstract will occupy the most space on most forms. Here, the abstractor must be given licence to express the ideas that he finds in the original in the most appropriate manner. Consistency can be achieved only in respect of special words such as abbreviations. Any mis-spellings, poor grammar and verbose phrasing and any other features that contravene good abstracting practice must be eliminated. The editor will also be concerned to achieve a uniform style of writing.

The last two categories of information, the indexing terms and further information, must also be reviewed. These data must have been recorded in the standard form for the publication and/or database. Indexing terms must have been drawn from a controlled list that is in use, and other details, such as the language of the original document, must be recorded in a standard form. For entries that are to be incorporated into an abstracts bulletin or publication that is basically arranged by alphabetical subject headings, these subject headings must be present. Section headings may be added by the editor at the final checking stage, or they may be assigned by the individual abstractor. If the editor is responsible for adding alphabetical subject section headings he can be more sure of uniformity in the categorization of entries.

Finally, then, it must lie with the editor to ensure that the submissions from individual contributors are legible. Whether entries are to be typed and directly duplicated or put into a computerized information-retrieval system they must be easily transcribed by the keyboard operator. In particular, any unusual or technical terms must be carefully written. Illegibility at this stage will lead to errors in the final product.

Some of the aspects of editorial control in the context of abstracting and indexing publications have been considered, but plainly the exact nature of the editor's duties depends upon the product and his working environment. An indexing or abstracting publication which is cumulated by computer, printed to a high standard and sold to an international market will plainly make very different demands from an in-house abstracting bulletin with only a few entries. Chapter 10 has considered some of the features of these two products.

Proofreading and copy preparation

Before a manuscript or copy can be typeset it must be marked up from a typographic specification which will suit it to typesetting by an appropriate composition method. The following represent some of the factors that might need to be specified:

- designations and sizes of typefaces and typefounts, special characters, rules and borders
- line length
- intercolumn spacing and interline spacing
- character and word spacing
- justification, indentation and hyphenation.

Marks must be used to designate most of these factors. The marks that are used in copy preparation may be the same marks as are used in proofreading.

Normally, before a manuscript is printed or duplicated in multiple copies the editor will be provided with printer's proofs or a master copy in order to check that they match his specification, and that the specification is in fact satisfactory. There are standard proofreading symbols. One set of such symbols is embodied in BS 5261:Part 1:1975(1983) *Recommendations for preparation of typescript copy for printing*, which lays some principles down, and Part 2:1976 *Specification for typographic requirements, marks for copy preparation and proof correction, proofing procedure*, which gives the proofreading symbols.

If computer typesetting is employed or if output is to be formatted with the aid of the output formatting devices available in most information-retrieval and database-management software packages, it will not be necessary to mark up printed text for typesetting. It will, however, still be necessary to code the text in the database for output in a style that is consistent with the provisions of the software package that is in use. This will usually involve specifying all of the items listed above, as well as page sizes and various other details.

FURTHER READING

This text lays the foundations for an appreciation of the principles and practice of abstracting and indexing. The student would profit by pursuing some of the topics introduced in this work further. Some books and periodical articles which may be usefully consulted are listed below. Many other equally valuable works have been omitted and, in particular, only a few periodical articles have been listed. The student is urged to scan appropriate periodicals for developments in the areas of abstracting, indexing, and abstracting and indexing products.

Periodicals which frequently contain contributions on these topics include:

Aslib proceedings
Catalogue and index
Database
Electronic library
Electronic publishing review
The indexer
Information age
Information processing and management
Information services and use
Information storage and retrieval
Information technology and libraries information world
Journal of documentation
Journal of information science
Journal of the American Society for Information Science
Online
Online review
Program
Special libraries
Vine

Abstracting
American National Standards Institute, *American national standard for writing abstracts*, New York, ANSI, 1971.
American Petroleum Institute (API), *Abstracts of refining literature:*

abstractors' manual, New York, API, 1969.

American Psychological Association, *Guide for volunteer abstractors*, Washington (D.C.), APA (undated).

The Anglo-American cataloguing rules (British text), 2nd edition, London, Library Association, 1979.

Ashworth, W., 'Abstracting', in *Handbook of special librarianship and information work*, 4th edition, London, Aslib, 1975, 124–52.

Ashworth, W., 'Abstracting as a fine art', *Information scientist*, 7, 1973, 43–53.

Bernier, C.L., 'Abstracts and abstracting', in *Encyclopedia of library and information science*, Vol.1, New York, Dekker, 1968, 16–38.

Borko, H. and Bernier, C.L., *Abstracting concepts and methods*, New York, Academic Press, 1975.

Borko, H. and Chatman, S., 'Criteria for acceptable abstracts: a survey of abstractors' instructions', *American documentation*, **14**, 1963, 149–60.

Chemical Abstracts Service, *Directions for abstractors*, 1971 Revision, Ohio State University, 1971.

Collison, R.L., *Abstracts and abstracting services*, Santa Barbara (California), ABC-Clio, 1971.

Educational Resources Information Center, 'ERIC guidelines for abstracting', in *ERIC operating manual*, Washington (D.C.), ERIC, 1967, Section 3.4.2.

Fidel, Raya, 'Writing abstracts for free-text searching', *Journal of Documentation*, **42** (1), March 1986, 11–21.

International Organisation for Standardisation, *Documentation: abstracts for publication and documentation*, Geneva, ISO, 1976.

International Atomic Energy Agency, *INIS: instructions for submitting abstracts*, Vienna, IAEA, 1971.

International Federation of Library Associations, International Office for UBC, *Standardisation activities of concern to libraries and national bibliographies*, London, IFLA Committee on Cataloguing, 1976.

Maizell, R.E., Smith, J.F. and Singer, T.E.R., *Abstracting scientific and technical literature: an introductory guide and text for scientists, abstractors and management*, New York, Wiley, 1971.

Mount, E., 'A national standard for bibliographic references', *Journal of the American Society for Information Science*, January 1977, 3–12.

Wagers, R., 'Effective searching in database abstracts', *Online*, 7 (5), 1983, 60–77.

Wainwright, J., *Standards used in bibliographic tape services: a comparison*, London, Aslib, 1974.

Wellisch, H.H., 'Documentation in source for library and information science', *Library resources and technical services*, **15**, 1971, 439–51.

Indexing

American National Standards Institute, *American national standard guidelines for thesaurus structure, construction and use*, New York, ANSI, 1974 (239, 19).

Aitchison, J., 'A classification as a source for a thesaurus: the Bibliographic Classification of H.E. Bliss as a source of thesaurus terms and structure', *Journal of documentation*, **42** (3), September 1986, 160–81.

Aitchison, J., *Thesaurus on youth: an integrated classification and thesaurus for youth affairs and related topics*, Leicester, National Youth Bureau, 1981.

Askew, C., *Thesaurus of consumer terms*, London, Consumers' Association; The Hague, International Organisation of Consumer Unions, 1979.

Austin, D., 'The development of PRECIS: a theoretical and technical history', *Journal of documentation*, March 1974, 47–102.

Austin, D., *PRECIS: a manual of concept analysis and subject indexing*, 2nd edition, London, British Library, Bibliographic Services Division, 1984.

Austin, D., 'PRECIS: an overview', *Libri*, **26**, 1976, 1–37.

Austin, D., 'The PRECIS system', in International PRECIS Workshop, University of Maryland, 1976. *The Precis index system: principles, applications and prospects*, edited by Hans Wellisch, New York, Wilson, 1977, 3–97.

Austin, D. and Digger, J.A., 'PRECIS: the PREserved Context Index System', *Library resources and technical services*, Winter 1977, 13–30.

Bakewell, K.G.B., 'The PRECIS indexing system', *The indexer,* **9** (4), October 1975, 160–6.

British Standards Institution, *BSI ROOT thesaurus*, 2nd edition, Milton Keynes, BSI, 1985.

British Standards Institution, *Guidelines for the establishment of monolingual thesauri*, BS 5723. London: BSI, 1979.

Campey, L.H., *Generating and printing indexes by computer*, London, Aslib, 1972 (Occasional Publication No 1).

Carrow, D. and Nugent, J., 'Comparison of free-text and index search capabilities in an operating information system', *Proceedings of the American Society for Information Science Annual Meeting,* **14** (2), 1977, 2–8.

Coates, E.J., *Subject catalogues: headings and structures*, London, Library Association, 1960.

Costello, J.C., 'Coordinate indexing', in *Rutgers series on systems for the intellectual organisation of information*, edited by S. Artandi, Rutgers State University Graduate School of Library Science,

1966 (No 7).

Cutter, S.A., *Rules for a dictionary catalogue*, 4th edition, Washington (D.C.), Government Printing Office, 1904.

Dubois, C.P.R., 'The use of thesauri in online retrieval', *Journal of information science*, **8** (2), 1984, 63–6.

Dykstra, M., *PRECIS: a primer*, London, British Library, Bibliographic Services Division, 1985.

English Electric Co. Ltd, *Thesaurofacet*, London, EEC, 1969.

Engineers Joint Council, *Thesaurus of engineering and scientific terms*, New York, EJC, 1967.

Feinberg, H., *Title derivative indexing techniques: a comparative study*, Los Angeles, Scarecrow Press, 1975.

Foskett, A.C., *The subject approach to information*, 4th edition, London, Bingley, 1982.

Foskett, D.J., 'Thesaurus', in *Encyclopedia of library and information science*, Vol.30, New York, Marcel Dekker, 1981.

Gilchrist, A., *The thesaurus in retrieval*, London, Aslib, 1971.

Gilchrist, A. and Aitchison, J., *Manual of thesaurus construction*, 2nd edition, London, Aslib, 1987.

Henzler, R.G., 'Free or controlled vocabularies: some statistical user-oriented evaluations of biomedical information systems', *International classification*, **5** (1), 1978, 21–6.

Hersey, D.F. et al, 'Comparison of on-line retrieval using free-text words and scientist indexing', in *The information conscious society: proceedings of the American Society for Information Science 33rd Annual Meeting, 11–15 October 1970, Philadelphia*, ASIS, Washington, 1970, 265–8.

Hersey, D.F. et al, 'Free text word retrieval and scientist indexing: performance profiles and costs', *Journal of documentation*, **27**, 1971, 1967–83.

Hunter, E.J. and Bakewell, K.G.B., *Cataloguing*, 2nd edition, London, Bingley, 1983.

INSPEC thesaurus, London, Institution of Electrical Engineers, 1987.

Indexers on indexing, edited by L. Harrod, New York, Bowker, 1978.

International Standards Organisation, *Guidelines for the establishment and development of monolingual thesauri*, Geneva, ISO, 1974.

INIS thesaurus, Vienna, International Atomic Energy Agency, 1974.

Kaiser, J., *Systematic indexing*, London, Pitman, 1911.

Keyword catalogues and the free language approach: papers based on a seminar held at Imperial College, London, 19 October 1983, edited by Philip Bryant, Bath, Bath University Library, 1985.

Knight, G.N., *Indexing: the art of*, London, Allen & Unwin, 1979.

Lancaster, F.W., *Information retrieval systems: characteristics, testing and evaluation*, New York, Wiley, 1968.

Lancaster, F.W., *Vocabulary control for information retrieval*, 2nd edition, Information Resources Press, 1986.

Markey, K. et al., 'An analysis of controlled vocabulary and free text search statements in online searches', *Online review,* **4** (3), 1980, 225–36.

Matthews, F.W. and Shillingford, A.D., 'Variations on KWIC', *Aslib proceedings,* **25** (4), April 1973, 140–52.

NASA thesaurus: Vol.1 Alphabetical listing: Vol.2 Access vocabulary, NASA, 1976.

Negus, A.E., 'Development of the Euronet Diane Common Command Language', in *Proceedings of the 3rd International Online Information Meeting, London, 4-6 December 1979,* Oxford, Learned Information, 1979, 95–8.

Raitt, D.I., 'Recall and precision devices in interactive bibliographic search and retrieval systems', *Aslib proceedings,* **32** (7/8), July/August, 1980, 281–301.

Smith, Inese A., 'Development of indexing systems at the National Youth Bureau', *Catalogue and index,* **73**, Summer 1984, 1–4.

Soergel, D., *Indexing languages and thesaurus: construction and maintenance,* Los Angeles, Melville, 1974.

Stein, D., et al., 'Full text online patent searching: results of a USPTO experiment', in *Proceedings of the Online '82 Conference, 1–3 November 1982, Atlanta, GA.,* Weston (CT), Online Inc., 1982, 289–94.

Subject headings for engineering, The Engineering Index Inc., New York, 1972.

Subject thesaurus for Bowker online databases, New York, London, Bowker, 1984.

Tenopir, C., 'Full text database retrieval performance', *Online review,* **9**, 1985, 149–60.

Tenopir, C., 'Searching *Harvard business review* online–lessons in searching a full text database', *Online,* **9**, 1985, 71–8.

Teskey, F.N., 'STATUS and integrated information systems', *Journal of documentation,* **36** (1), March 1980, 33–9.

Thesaurus of metallurgical terms, 5th edition, Metals Park, Ohio, American Society for Metals, 1981.

Thesaurus of psychological terms, 4th edition, Hyattsville (Maryland), American Psychological Association, 1986.

Townley, H.M. and Gee, R.D., *Thesaurus-making: grow your own word stock,* London, Deutsch, 1980.

Van Rijsbergen, C.J., *Information retrieval,* London, Butterworths, 1975.

Vernon, K.D.C. and Lang, V., *The London classification of business studies,* 2nd edition.

Vickery, B.C., 'Knowledge representation: a brief review', *Journal of documentation*, **42** (3), September 1986, 145–59.

Vickery, B.C., *Techniques of information retrieval*, London, Butterworths, 1970.

Watters, C.R. et al., 'Integration of menu retrieval and Boolean retrieval from a full-text database', *Online review*, **9**, 1985, 391–401.

Indexing and abstracting products

Ashford, J. and Matkin, D., *Studies in the application of free-text package systems*, London, Library Association, 1982 (Case studies in library automation).

Barker, F.H. and Taylor, F.J., 'The use of the BASIS database management system to produce a highly current technocommercial database', *Program*, **19**, 1985, 322–38.

Burton, P.F., *Microcomputers in library and information services: an annotated bibliography*, Aldershot, Gower, 1986.

Collier, M., *Microcomputer software for information management: an annotated bibliography*, Aldershot, Gower, 1986.

Collier, M., *Microcomputer software for information management: case studies*, Aldershot, Gower, 1986.

Deunette, J.V. et al., *Going online*, London, Aslib, 1984.

Directory of online databases (quarterly), New York, Cuadra/Elsevier.

EUSIDIC database guide, Oxford, Learned Information, 1983.

Fenichel, C.H. and Hogan, T.H., *Online searching: a primer*, 2nd edition, Medford (N.J.), Learned Information, 1984.

Ford, S. and Mark, R., 'ADLIB–its use by the Greater London Council Research Library', *Program*, **18**, 1984, 339–50.

Hall, J.L., *Online bibliographic databases*, 4th edition, London, Aslib, 1986.

Henry, W.M. et al., *Online searching: an introduction*, London, Butterworths, 1980.

Hoover, R.E. (ed.), *The library and information manager's guide to online services*, White Plains (N.Y.), Knowledge Industry Publications, 1980.

Houghton, B. and Convey, J., *Online information retrieval systems*, 2nd edition, London, Bingley, 1984.

Lambert, S., *Online: a guide to America's leading information services*, New York, Microsoft Press, 1985.

Leggate, P., 'Computer based current awareness services', *Journal of documentation*, **31** (2), 1975, 93–115.

Lancaster, F.W. and Fayen, E.G., *Information retrieval on-line*, Los Angeles, Melville, 1973.

Meadows, C. and Cochrane, P., *Basics of online searching*, Chichester, Wiley, 1981.

'Online information retrieval bibliography (1985), 8th update', *Online review,* **9**, 1985, S1—S88.

Practical current awareness services from libraries, edited by Tom Whitehall, Aldershot, Gower, 1986.

Proceedings of the International Online Information Meetings, 5th, 6th, 7th, 8th and 9th, 1981—5, Oxford, Learned Information.

Raitt, D.I. (ed.), *An introduction to online information systems,* Oxford, Learned Information, 1985.

Rowley, J.E., 'Local current awareness services in industrial libraries', *Aslib proceedings,* **31** (10), October 1979, 476—84.

Rowley, J.E., 'Locally produced current awareness services', *Aslib proceedings,* **31** (6), June 1979, 284—95.

Text retrieval: a directory of software, edited by Robert Kimberley, with an introduction by Jennifer Rowley, 2nd edition, Aldershot, Gower, 1987.

Williams, M.E. (ed.), *Computer readable databases—a directory and data source book,* Vols. 1 and 2, 4th edition, North Holland, Amsterdam, North Holland, 1985.

INDEX

A Topography of Cataloguing:

showing the most important landmarks, communications and perilous places

Mary Piggott

1988; 304pp; 0 85365 758 0

From time to time an author in the field of library science comes foward who can combine expert knowledge of a complex subject with lucidity of expression. Rare indeed is the author who also possesses an agreeable and entertaining literary style, endowing exposition with the pleasant readability of the essay. Mary Piggott is just such an author and her book is just such a work.

Mary Piggott conveys in 'The Topography of Cataloguing' all that her 27 years as a lecturer in Cataloguing and Bibliography at the School of Library, Archive and Information Science, University College London has taught her about the need to widen and deepen a student's knowledge of how language, social organization and intellectual communication determine the decisions that the cataloguer makes. In this context there is discussion of such basic issues as 'Are catalogues necessary?' – 'In an age of centralized cataloguing why should all librarians learn to catalogue?' – 'What are standards and why are they necessary?'

The underlying problems of language – together with the importance of its precise and consistent use – are also examined in the context of both descriptive and subject cataloguing.

This book sets out in general terms the problems and solutions that confront the cataloguer. It does not consider specific materials and their treatment, neither does it refer, except in rare instances, to specific codes and rules. Such a necessary continuation forms the matter of the companion volume; *.The Cataloguer's Way: from document receipt to document retrieval* (ISBN 0 85365 768 8).